L.H

Yesterday on the Hill

Yesterday on the Hill

Memories of Colehill

George Sadler

THE STANHOPE PRESS

© George Sadler 1996

First published in Great Britain 1996
by Stanhope Press, Colehill
Wimborne, Dorset BH21 2PR

Typeset in Sabon by The Typesetting Bureau
Allen House, East Borough, Wimborne, Dorset
Printed in Great Britain by
TJ Press (Padstow) Ltd, Padstow, Cornwall

ISBN 0 9528295 0 9

Contents

Acknowledgements

I could not have written this book without the help of a great number of the village people, many of them still living on Colehill or in the neighbourhood, with a handful of exiles now in distant parts. Not all of the villagers named here are, sad to say, still alive to receive this mark of my gratitude.

For their invaluable assistance in many ways, especially for giving their time to recall anecdotes of "Yesterday on the Hill", and to some for the loan of photographs, I must record my thanks to the following: Mrs Audrey Bartram, Reg Batchelor, Miss Gillian Bell, John Billington, Frank Bray, Charlie and Phyllis Budden, David Bullen, Miss Frances Burden, John Butler, Mrs Louisa Butler, Tom Chissell, Miss Lily Christopher, Bill Cole, the Misses Jeannette and Ruby Coombes, Mrs Phyllis Coombs, Mrs Kathy Curtler, John Dacombe, Mrs Ellen Dean, Jack Douch, Les Douch, Mrs Sylvia Frampton, Mrs Margaret Giles, Rev John Goodall, Col George Gray, Roger Guttridge, Bert Habgood, Miss Brenda Habgood, E.F.J. Hawkins, Dudley Hebdige, Christine Holder, Mrs Holloway, Mrs Doris Jeanes, Maurice Jenkins, Andrew Jones, Mrs Jackie Kirby, Harry Langer, Donald Legg, Mrs Winifred Lethbridge, Mrs Valerie Marshall, A.J. Maton, Mrs Dolly Maund, Mrs Pam McClintock, Andrew Mears, Maurice Moody, Alec Moore, Pat O'Hara, Eric Osman, Dennis Ould, A. Packer, Mrs Pinchbeck, Steve Rawlings, Patrick Reeves, Mrs Iris Rocksborough-Smith, Mrs Rene Sawtell, Miss Betty Shiner, Ken Shiner, George Solly, John Solly, Bill Stevens, Mrs Stewart, Mrs Margaret Walker, Garth Watson, Harold Wheeler, Arthur and Molly Whiley, Mrs Vera Wigmore, Derek Williams, Mrs Vera Williams, Wilfred Williams, Eric Winchester and Derrick Wollen.

I am very grateful to my family for their support, encouragement and practical help in so many ways; and I would especially like to thank Des Curtis for his time and expertise on technical matters.

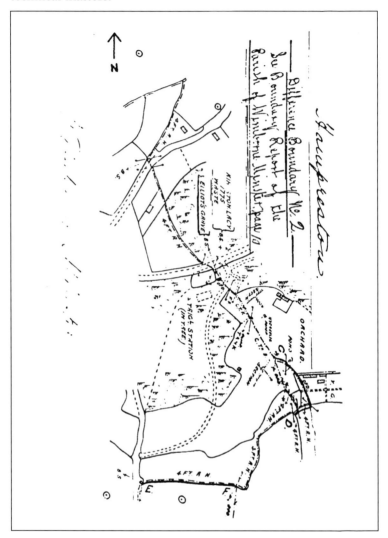

1 Part of the Park Homer Estate, taken from a map of about 1885. Lonnen Road runs diagonally on the left-hand side; Middlehill Road is in the centre; and Park Homer Road and Park Homer Drive now occupy most of the southern half of the map.

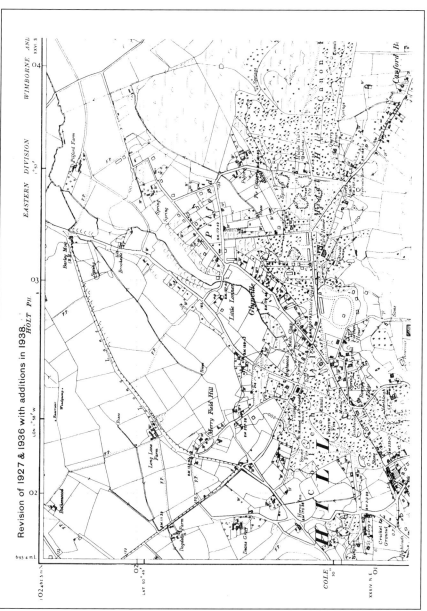

2 1927 Ordnance Survey, with additions up to 1938. Already, part of the future shape of Colehill is indicated by the dotted lines marking Park Homer Road.

[3]

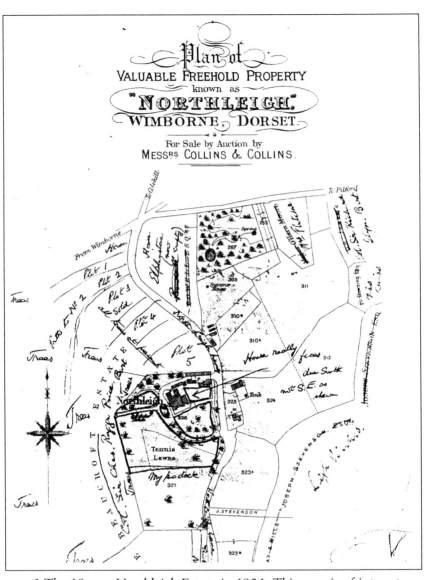

3 *The 18-acre Northleigh Estate in 1921. This map is of interest as showing the owners of adjoining property, much of which has clearly changed hands during the tenure of the Stringer family. The amendments appear to date from the late 1940s, and were probably made by Colin Stringer.*

[4]

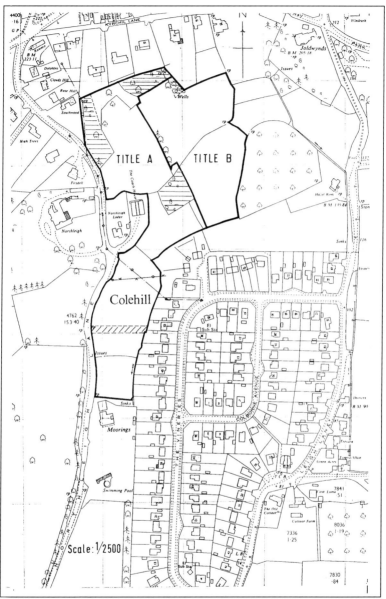

4 The remaining ten acres of the Northleigh Estate were sold in 1972 by the joint owners, Colin Stringer and Peter and Joan Alliss. The House and its buildings across the road had already been sold, as had the old Plantation with its frontage to Kyrchil Lane. The Vineries had metamorphosed from glass to bricks and mortar.

Introduction
The Salubrious Suburb

"There is more research to be done, and more history to be written". With these prophetic words, I brought to a conclusion my book on the history of Colehill, *Village on the Hill*, researched and written over a period of many years and published in 1992.

Regrettably, my efforts to trace Legan Lodge or William Noble's ancestor who lived there more than a century and a half ago have remained fruitless; on the other hand, my history has met with such an enthusiastic response and produced so much "feed-back" – in the form both of information and photographs – that I am encouraged to write more about the story of the village and its inhabitants for the benefit of posterity, as well as for those of us who enjoy reading about the old times.

I have heard, or read, Colehill described as "The Salubrious Suburb". And one cannot, certainly on the face of it, quarrel with such an epithet. Perched on the hill above Wimborne, where many of the present population work, while still others commute daily to Poole and Bournemouth, it had clearly proved, as far back as the middle of the last century, to be an attractive place, among the pinewoods, for the well-to-do to build their new mansions, Bells, Northleigh, Onslow, and the rest, and to rub shoulders with neighbours from the landed gentry, such as the Greatheds, at Uddens.

The emergence of Colehill as a *village* rather than a scattering of thatched, mud-built cottages – which it had been for previous centuries – clearly arose from the influx of the "new aristocracy" in the second half of the nineteenth century, and the need, having built their houses, using largely material from the local brickworks, for tradesmen and domestic servants to attend to their requirements. Thus it was that a self-contained community sprang up, quite distinct from its larger neighbour down the hill, to achieve the status of a village, both in fact and in official recognition.

It was created a civil parish in its own right, under the Local Government Act of 1894, after a brief spell as the southern ward of the Parish of Holt. An anomaly that preserved the jurisdiction of Hampreston over the eastern half of the village – corresponding roughly to the land owned by the Greatheds, and including, significantly, the village school at Middle Hill – was rectified in 1913. The ecclesiastical parish, whose boundaries vary considerably from those of the civil parish, was formed in 1903, although the Anglican Church, St Michael and All Angels, dates from 1893. The predecessor of the present church, the "Iron Church", had been erected, not far away, in 1881. The Methodists were even earlier, having erected their first, mud-built, church in 1855.

Earlier still were *The Horns* and *The Barley Mow*, both of which date back some hundreds of years. All three of the village hostelries lie on its outskirts, and the third, the *Sir Winston Churchill* is a relative newcomer.

Other manifestations of the emerging village were the coming of the village school, Middle Hill School, in 1865, and, no doubt in many respects socially, as well as geographically, at the centre of the village, the Post Office, built in 1897, with Frank Barrett as Postmaster.

Sporting and social institutions, among them the Cricket Club, so successful down the years, the Football Club and the Women's Institute, all started in the early years of this century, have all helped to proclaim the separate identity of Colehill as a village, not merely a pleasant suburban appendage of Wimborne.

These "bare bones" of the history of the village are necessary to give some sort of background to what follows: but they must suffice. It is not my purpose here to *rewrite* the history of the village, although I have, here and there, brought it rather more up-to-date. I have been helped in compiling this account by many individuals, whose roots in the village go much deeper than mine; indeed, without them, this record could never have appeared: I have merely been the scribe. I have recorded my acknowledgements, and I hope my list is complete, elsewhere in this book.

I

Below The Hill

The southern slopes of Colehill still retain, even in the last decade of the twentieth century, something of a rural appearance, although many acres of pasture have been swallowed up in residential building in the last 30 years. However, cattle have grazed in the remaining fields in the recent past, and a number of horses, as well as deer, foxes and rabbits, still do.

The slopes facing the mid-day sun might seem as good a place as any on which to grow grapes; and, indeed, a family historian has brought to light that wine was made from vineyards behind her home in Leigh Lane by Mary Ann Longman in the early years of this century; on a much larger scale commercially, the Leigh Vinery was begun at about the same time; eventually, eight and a half acres of the land between Leigh Lane and Northleigh Lane were covered by glasshouses and the business flourished until the early 'sixties. Leigh Vineries was started by Josiah Quertier, a Jerseyman, growing grapes, peaches, cucumbers and, especially in the years between the wars, vast quantities of tomatoes, when Mackay's Glasshouse Properties Ltd, originally a partnership of Captain Frank Forbes Mackay, a Scot, and A.R. Wills, became the owners. Wills left the business, being succeeded by Murray, and he, in turn, was followed by Captain George Cummings, who managed the business in its later years, while Mackay continued in office as something of a "sleeping" partner. Flowers such as arum lilies were also cultivated latterly.

There were two smaller businesses which adjoined Mackay's, at the bottom of the Vineries, extending the area of glass still further. One of these was owned by John McGhie – Scotsmen seem to have been much in evidence in the district in this line of trade – whose home, Ashley House, in Northleigh Lane,

Leigh Vineries c. 1930. Four thatched cottages abut on the eastern side of Leigh Lane – only one now remains. The railway clips the bottom right-hand corner of the picture. Looking north-eastwards, the view extends beyond the hill, towards Clayford and Verwood.

abutted on to his nursery, where Italian prisoners-of-war were employed during the 1939-45 war; and the other by Captain Nichols, whose business, next-door, adjoined his home, Fairfield House.

The 1901 Ordnance map shows clearly that the original Leigh "Vinery" consisted of a single row of three glasshouses, covering about four acres, and stretching from the manager's house in Leigh Lane across to the back of Quertier's house, Moorings, in Northleigh Lane – the lower *even* numbered houses in Colborne Avenue now cover the site. The manager's house also accomodated the office, and adjoined what remained the entrance to the Vineries in later years when the glass covered area was substantially extended both north and south of the original. Moorings continued its close connection with the Vineries after Quertier's time, becoming the home of Mackay and, later, of Cummings.

At its peak, in the late thirties, just before the war, there were about 50 employees engaged in the business, and as many as 60 worked there after the war; it was one of the largest firms in the district, and certainly the biggest on Colehill. The foreman was George Fish, and he was succeeded by Mac James. The boilers supplying hot water to the glasshouses were stoked by Percy Fry, "Pompey" Portsmouth and Maurice Jenkins. Portsmouth, whose home, a thatched cottage in Leigh Lane, very close to his work, fell into disrepair after the war, and was demolished, is remembered by some of his workmates as continually whistling as he went about his duties. Jenkins, whose father, Harry, had also been a stoker at the Vineries, is perhaps more widely remembered in his later career as the Verger at Wimborne Minster. The market for the fruit and vegetables extended throughout much of the country, produce being despatched both by railway, via Wimborne Station, and by road, with lorries travelling as far afield as Birmingham and Nottingham.

The company maintained a sports club, fielding cricket and football elevens, who played at fields adjoining the associated nurseries at Stourbank in Ham Lane, Little Canford, before the

Leigh Vineries c. 1947. Harry Sheppard with three Land Girls (l. to r.) Winnie Lawes, Pat Steel and Beryl Chalkley.

Above *Propogating section, with (l. to r.) Harry Sheppard, Frank Bray and George Lee.*

Left *Frank Bray.*

Firm's entry for Wimborne Carnival, with Morris Commercial lorry as "float". The figures include Ken Keeping, Frank Bray, Joy Steel, Pat Steel, Violet Joyce, Winnie Lawes, Beryl Chalkley, Violet Legg, May Clark and Ruth Wyatt.

The Vineries Football Club at their ground at Ham Lane, Little Canford 1937-8. Back row (l. to r.): Rogers, Tom Pitt, Monty Ellis, Frank Cheeseman, Percy Hunt, Bob Homer, Stan Hart and Mac James; front (l. to r.): Bert Whitmarsh, Jimmy James, Percy Loader, Clarence Cousins and Wilf Cousins.

war. The tomatoes and cucumbers of their working lives were reflected on the football pitch with the team's red and green shirts. Indoor games, darts, snooker and so on, were catered for in premises in East Borough, Wimborne, and there was a tennis court, which later became a coal dump, adjoining the glasshouses in Leigh Lane. Shortly before the outbreak of war, Cummings insisted on all the employees enlisting in the Territorial Army, and they were replaced, when they were called up, by women. A substantial staff was maintained during the war, when a large number of Land Girls were employed.

The houses at the top of the Vineries were erected in 1948 for the firm's employees; and Lindsey Kerr took over the management of the nursery business. This finally collapsed, several years after the war, for a variety of reasons, including an invasion of eel-worm, which ruined the tomato crop, an unfortunate and ill-timed decision to convert the boilers from coal to oil-firing, at the time of the Suez crisis of 1956, with the consequent shortage of oil; and competition from the Channel Islands. A new housing estate was built on the site of Leigh Vineries in the early 'sixties. Kerr converted his manager's

Drovers Cottage, Leigh Lane c. 1960.

house into a general store, which served the newcomers for a few years, before closing, like so many of its kind, in the face of competition from the new supermarkets. The reservoir supplying the Vineries, in use during the war as an Emergency Water Supply, survived for several years after the demolition of the glasshouses, and became something of an attraction to the children of the neighbourhood; the water was 30 feet deep, and the tank was not without its perils, as more than one adventurous youngster can testify!

The eastern side of Leigh Lane does, however, retain something of a pastoral aspect, but only one of the several thatched cottages which once stood there now remains. Of the others, Drovers Cottage, regrettably severely damaged by fire recently, and now demolished, was once the home of the Moody family, well-known in the village, and its name gave at least a hint of the occupation of its original tenant, when agriculture flourished in the area. Further down the hill stood another thatched cottage, destroyed during the war in an air raid. This was the birth-place of Alec Moore, a chorister at St Michael's Church now for close on 70 years, and descendant of one of the oldest Colehill families. His great-grandfather, Alfred Moore, was a gardener at Beaucroft House, having previously been the coachman there to Mrs Lees, and later worked at the Leigh Vineries. Alec's father perished in the Great War and is remembered on the village War Memorial. His widow remarried, her second husband being David Cobb, and so establishing a relationship with the brick-making family. Another victim of the war, Bill Cole, survived that terrible conflict, having served in the Dorset Regiment from 1916 to 1918. He did not escape unscathed, however, and, at the age of 92, remembered his younger days vividly. He recalled being three days and nights on the march in the advance from the Somme, near Arras, before being wounded. A machine-gun bullet in his shoulder and one in his back were removed; but the bullet in his liver remained, and stayed in his body for the rest of his life. He lived to be 95. One recollection of this veteran of the horrors of the Western Front, which afforded him much amusement, was being frightened while on leave by a white dog which jumped out of a hedge. The land "Fit for

Heroes" rewarded him with £1 per week when he was demobbed, before he was able to find work. A bricklayer by trade, he found part-time work, during spells of unemployment, at the Vineries.

Across the fields, cultivated until recent times, as part of Brookside Farm, by Henry and Jesse Purchase, and then by Tom Chissell, to the east of Leigh Lane and running more or less parallel with it, a series of hedges mark a very ancient boundary, that between the Kingston Lacy and the Uddens Estates. The same boundary served, in more modern times, to divide the civil parishes of Colehill and Hampreston before the eastern part of the village was transferred to Colehill in 1913. The Ordnance Survey maps of the last century show the boundary with the legend "4 ft. R.H."; the Ordnance Survey history discloses that this inscription indicates that the precise boundary lies four feet from the root of the adjoining hedge.

During the 1939-1945 war, tanks were kept on the Vineries, and the local boys would earn a penny or two helping the soldiers polish the vehicles. Men of the Middlesex Regiment, the King's Own Dragoon Guards, the Tank Corps and the 10th Royal Hussars were quartered in the district, any house, large or small, with available room being requisitioned for billets. The Officers' Mess was in Beaucroft Lane, and the men used to feed at *The Jockey House*.

The London and South Western Railway Company built their line from Southampton via Wimborne to Dorchester in 1847, cutting across the northern part of Leigh Common. The company agreed to compensate the commoners for their loss of part of the land, but questions were being asked, as late as 1875, at the Vestry Meeting of Wimborne Minster, as to what had become of the money, and suggesting that, when found, it should be used for the repair of Leigh Road. The railway, promoted by the Wimborne lawyer, Charles Castleman, was dubbed "Castleman's Corkscrew" on account of its tortuous route across the New Forest and on to Poole. Cottages were built to house those responsible for manning the level crossings, and several of these small square bungalows still survive locally, including those where Canford Bottom and Hayes Lane crossed the railway. The crossing-keeper's cottage in Leigh Lane is something of a curiosity in that there is now no evidence of the crossing itself. However, Leigh Lane did at one time continue down the hill, crossing Leigh Common diagonally, and its original course can still be traced today, along the gravel track, now interrupted by the southern approach to the Northleigh Lane railway bridge. Leigh Lane, with the coming of the railway, was provided with its level crossing, to continue across the Common, and was not diverted to the bridge, two hundred yards to the west, carrying Northleigh Lane, until several years later. This bridge and the crossing-keeper's cottages constitute the few remnants of what was at one time the busy main-line railway linking London with Poole and Dorchester, and which survived as a branch line until 30 years ago.

The line was exceptionally busy during the 1939 war, when it was a common sight to see goods trains hauling as many as 30 trucks laden with tanks. Bombs damaged the railway during one air raid, one causing a large crater, disrupting traffic, while others fell harmlessly in the neighbouring Church Moor Copse.

The erection of the Northleigh Lane bridge, clearly an afterthought following the building of the railway, together with its approach roads, must have been a monumental undertaking, no doubt involving much manual labour and horse power, in those days of rudimentary machines. The somewhat flimsy wire fencing and its associated concrete posts which line the approach road to the bridge from Leigh Road are said to date from the time of the original works. Half-way down this slope, on the eastern side, stood the old pound, in which the hayward of Leigh would confine cattle and other livestock, not belonging to commoners, grazing illegally on the Common.

The coming of the line brought quite a little army of railway employees, several of whom came to live in the houses beside the Common. One of the old thatched cottages there, all later demolished, was occupied in the 1930s by George Cox, the local chimney-sweep. He had the reputation of being rather choosy as to his customers. Access to unlimited quantities of soot enabled him to liberally fertilize his garden, which has since borne produce in abundance.

His unfortunate wife, Kate, became familiar in the neighbourhood as the victim of periodic convulsions. George's household also included his brother, Harry, a dairyman who regularly attended the weekly Wimborne market to milk the cows, as an employee of Jesse Purchase, of Brookside Farm. The 1891 census records William Bailey as a chimney sweep living on Leigh Common, with a ten-year-old step-son, Frederick Cox, from whom, perhaps, George was descended, and, if the same cottage, veritable mountains of soot must have accumulated!

"Granny" Willis was one resident at Leigh Common, who will be remembered by young mothers during the years of the second German war, as she acted as the local unofficial midwife. The thatched cottages survived until 1960, with few modern amenities, and were then demolished, being replaced by a row of bungalows on more or less the same site. One is now occupied by Donald Legg, born in one of the neighbouring cottages before the war. He can recall the conditions in the old cottages: the outside privy, but no mains drainage; no gas; no electricity; the outside tap, in front of the cottage, to obtain domestic water from the main. He remembers, too, the arrival of the Americans during the war, and their off-duty games of baseball on the Common. It was not an unusual sight to see the American "Flying Jeeps" (as their light Piper Cub aeroplanes were colloquially known) landing in and taking off from a field beside Leigh Road.

Leigh Common, part of the Deanery Estate, owned by the Hanham family, is of considerable antiquity, and is mentioned in Manorial records as long ago as 1774. In more recent years, with the creation of the modern system of local government, it became disputed territory between the parishes of Wimborne and Colehill, and, similarly, between Wimborne Minster Urban District and the Rural District of Wimborne and Cranborne. Rubbish-tipping and encampments of gypsies were causes of concern in the early years of this century, but the major problem exercising the authorities was the fact that Wimborne seems to have been draining its sewage into Leigh Pond. These matters were eventually resolved, after much acrimonious argument, and Leigh Common has become something of a very pleasant nature reserve, with a population of rabbits at play, and moorhens nesting on a sweet-smelling Leigh Pond. Snipe, owls, grass snakes and sand lizards made their home on the Common 50 years ago.

This was the scene of a traffic accident in 1929, when a Hants and Dorset bus, being driven furiously along what was then known as Ringwood Road, overturned and finished up in the Pond. Motor bus companies were at that time in fierce competition for passengers, and a "price war" was accompanied by some reckless driving.

Leigh, as a place-name, is recorded as long ago as Saxon times, and preserved its separate identity as a Tithing down the years. An entry in the annals of the Wimborne Minster Vestry refers to an Inquisition post mortem of Thomas Hanam (as the family name was spelt at the time), Sergeant-at-Law, dated in the 36th year of the reign of the first Elizabeth. This mentions "The Manor of Lie alias Leigh", which seems to be conclusive evidence for the correct – certainly the original – pronunciation of the name.

It seems clear, from old documents, that this part of Colehill, and that on the western slopes, that is to say, those parts adjoining Wimborne, were the earliest parts of the village to be settled. The Woodward Survey of 1775, for example, records Richard King's Close "near Leigh Turnpike" and Sir William Hanham as the freeholder of 117 acres "round Vincecombe, Leigh Farm, Great and Little Coneygar". The name "Vincecombe" had vanished a century later from the map of the Hanham Estate, although the meadow called Coneygar was still marked. Leigh Farm, in the 1870s, had been divided into "Upper" Leigh Farm, extending from north of the railway to the banks of the River Stour in the south, and "Lower" Leigh Farm, further to the east, which extended from Leigh Common southwards to the river. They were separated by a piece of land sold, in 1822, by William Dean (who had, presumably, purchased it from the Hanham Estate) to George Hatchard. This piece of arable land was called "Eighteen Acres", although its actual extent was rather less than that, and its subsequent interesting history is recorded in the Deeds of a property on part of the land which have been made available through the kindness of its present owner, Derek Williams. Hatchard farmed on a large scale, employing as many as 20 farm-hands, mainly near his home at Deans Grove, where he had a considerable acreage.

John Hatchard inherited Eighteen Acres from George – probably his father – and when John died, in 1882, it passed to *his* son, John Frederick Hatchard; and from him, in 1922, to his wife, Eleanora. The 1891 census records John Mayo as a dealer and farmer at Leigh Farm, presumably as a tenant, with Alfred Osman, the manager of the Wimborne Gas Works, as his neighbour at Gas Works House. Leigh Farm, on the site of the erstwhile "Upper" Farm, still extended from the railway to the river, as it continued to do until the middle years of this century. By the 1890s, the farm was occupied by the four Woodman Brothers – James, William, John and Henry – as tenants, who were successors to an earlier leaseholder, Monkton. In the year following her husband's death, Eleanora Hatchard sold the freehold to the Woodmans. George Purchase, of Brookside Farm, bought Eighteen Acres in 1926, and it is clear from the Deeds at this time that there was an intention of building houses on the part of the land with a frontage to Leigh Road. Indeed, one house, Danesbury, bearing a plaque with the initials "G. P." and the year "1926" was immediately built. None of the other houses originally envisaged was built for nearly 40 years afterwards; as to the subsequent annals of Danesbury, the only point of historic interest was the sale by Miss Helen Purchase in 1940 of a plot of land from her garden, with a frontage to Leigh Road, to the War Department. This is now the headquarters of the Wimborne Squadron of the Air Training Corps, which has inherited the little colony of Nissen huts which mushroomed on the site more than 50 years ago. These originally were in use by the Army as a supply depot.

As for the rest of Eighteen Acres and the adjoining Leigh Farm, Brook Road now runs through it, the Brook Road Industrial Estate occupies part of the river frontage, and the Flight Refuelling factory has spilled over into the remainder. Leigh Farm has contracted to the north of Leigh Road, farmed now by the sisters, the Misses Ruby and Jeannette Coombes, who have followed in the footsteps of their father, Edgar Coombes. Coombes, one of a large family of West Dorset

Leigh Pond and The Jockey House c. 1930.

The Jockey House c. 1930.

farmers, purchased the property in 1927, and, at first, the family lived in the old farm-house, a building of some antiquity, known sometimes as Leigh Manor House. The family moved to a newly erected house fronting Leigh Road in 1930. Their old home is now converted into flats and the old thatched stable is now Ken Wentworth's workshop for the repair of motor cars.

Leigh Common c. 1930. "Jockey Pond" is the name given here for Leigh Pond.

LEIGH COMMON. *probably about the turn of the century. The narrow, gravelled road is Ringwood Road, now called Leigh Road; the thatched building on the left is the "Horse and Jockey" inn – which later became "The Jockey House"; what later became Baldwin's bakery bears the name "Hatchard" on its wall: and, beyond, open country – Leigh Farm – separates Leigh Common from Wimborne.*

The land to the south was sold as was that to the west, the site of the houses built along Leigh Road in the 1930s. On the other hand, Coombes expanded to the north, beyond the railway line, purchasing Greenclose Farm – part of the old Hanham Estate, including the meadow known as Coneygar, up the hill beside Beaucroft Lane. The sisters continued farming when their father died in 1949, maintaining a dairy herd, and supplying Bolton's Dairy in Ferndown with "gold-top" milk. The farm is perhaps unique – certainly one of very few in Britain – still using the old-fashioned churns.

Ringwood Road, renamed Leigh Road more than 40 years ago, has been a highway since Roman times. It follows the line, or very close to the line, of the route linking Badbury Rings with Winchester. In more modern times, under the management of the Ringwood, Longham and Leigh Turnpike Trust, whose tollgate was at Leigh Common, it was the road taken by the stage coaches and the Royal Mails from London on their way to Wimborne and Poole.

Prior to the opening of the Wimborne by-pass road, Leigh Road was a part of the A31 trunk road. Less than a mile to the east of Leigh Common, the road mysteriously changes its name to "Wimborne Road West", and a prominent notice proclaims "Ferndown": a source, no doubt, of much confusion to strangers, as Ferndown in fact lies three miles further on. However, this is the modern boundary of the civil parishes of Colehill and Ferndown; more than that, it is the much more ancient boundary of the Kingston Lacy Estate, dating back certainly to 1590, when its "Perambulation" was surveyed, and probably even earlier.

Across the road from Leigh Pond – which, at the turn of the century, appears to have covered more than a quarter of an acre and abutted on to the highway – stood a thatched public house, with cobb walls, *The Horse and Jockey*, dating from the twelfth century. The inn sign portrayed a brown racehorse with its jockey wearing a yellow shirt with red spots. Frederick Welch was keeping the inn in 1841, and was succeeded by Joseph Dinneth 20 years later. J. J. Pearce has left a written record of the demise of the inn. "It was my auntie, a Mrs Luccombe, that lost the licence for selling beer on a Sunday about 1895. It was never used as an inn again."

The premises reopened after the Great War as *The Jockey House*, one of the so-called "Road Houses" fashionable at the time, when motoring was becoming popular. B. Willis was the original licensee, but Major Frank Hyde had taken over by 1935. In 1939, when Philip Richardson had become the owner, it was known as *The Jockey House and 12th Century Club* and had become a Night Club, where the "smart set" of Bournemouth and the neighbourhood enjoyed themselves. Leigh Pond was known at one time as the Jockey Pond, and a photograph of the time, taken from the road, shows the Pond, with cattle grazing on the Common beyond, and the railway line, curving round from the Northleigh Lane bridge towards Leigh Arch on the left. Contemporary photographs show the close proximity of a still substantial Leigh Pond to the highway, with, across the road, standing outside the night club, the life-like figure of a jockey on a white horse, just about to pass the winning post. This wooden carving became an attraction for the local lads, who would climb up and sit astride, behind the jockey – no doubt when no-one was watching!

The Jockey House did not survive the war, falling victim to the depredations, following its requisition by the military, of British and American soldiers, and, beyond repair, was allowed to crumble away, with the assistance of the inevitable vandals. Only the dance hall of the former night club, behind the main premises, remained. However, the name of the former hostelry has been perpetuated in the adjoining Jockey Cottages.

There seems to have been some confusion in the memories of local people about the demise of *The Jockey House*: vandalism was certainly a contributory factor, as well as sheer neglect after it had been released from Government control. It has been alleged that it was destroyed by fire, during an air raid. This, however, seems incorrect, and memories have transferred the fire, caused by incendiary bombs, to *The Jockey House*, from its actual location, no more than a hundred yards away, at Hope Cottage.

A rather amusing story associated with this incident –

amusing after a gap of 50 years, but far from funny at the time – was that both the Wimborne and the Ferndown Fire Brigades turned out to deal with the blaze. The Ferndown Brigade was first on the scene, having covered the four miles from their station considerably more quickly than their colleagues from Wimborne, one mile away. Having reached the fire, so the story goes, the Ferndown people discovered that the "incident" was not within their "territory", and so did nothing, watching the fire consume the building. Another version of the same story, somewhat reminiscent of Robb Wilton's comic wartime sketches on the radio, reverses the roles of the two fire brigades.

Twenty years were to elapse before another licensed house opened in the vicinity, several hundred yards further to the east, and on the opposite side of the road. The *Sir Winston Churchill*, originally to have been called *The Commoners*, opened with Jack Smith, formerly of *The Barley Mow*, on the far side of the hill, as its landlord. A later licensee was that Derek – more familiarly "Dixie" – Williams, who had grown up on Leigh Common, and who, as previously noted, has come back in his retirement to live nearby.

The Common has had other commercial connections down the years. Henry Farrant had a bakery not far from *The Jockey House* before the Great War, and Benjamin Saiby had been a baker here in the closing years of the last century. Some 25 years after Farrant moved up the hill to start his carrier's business in the early 'twenties, Ted Baldwin, who had worked in his father's bakery business – only a few doors from Farrant's garage in Wimborne Road – moved in the opposite direction and set up on his own as a baker in Farrant's old bakehouse, which had become empty. The premises remained a bakery throughout the war and for about 20 years afterwards. Baldwin sold the business to Jack Lockyer in 1948, and, from him, it passed to Tom Lockyer.

Herbert Cullen later turned the premises into a cafe, which it has remained under subsequent owners, Barry Lawrence, Janet Jones and the present proprietors, Martyn and Kathy Curtler, and now appropriately named "The Old Bakehouse", and still preserving, on the east wall, Baldwin's mural, dating

from 1941, advertising "The Thoro'bre(a)d Baker". This replaced an earlier sign, still there in Baldwin's time, bearing the name "Hatchard" – no doubt that same Farmer Hatchard who had owned the adjoining Eighteen Acres a hundred years previously. There was a registered slaughter-house, run by William Loader, near the Common in 1939, standing behind the bakery in a side turning from Leigh Road; Arthur Loader inherited the business from his father, and eventually, in 1961, sold it to Jack and Percy Strange. The business finally closed and the abattoir was demolished. J. Tucker and Son had a market garden, beside the slaughter-house, and Thomas Moore was a poultry farmer at "Leighbrook".

Left: William Loader c. 1935.

Below: William Loader, c. 1935, standing beside his pony's head, with one of his sons in the trap.

[26]

Brian Stringer, c. 1935, in his MG, outside Northleigh House.

The old dance hall of *The Jockey House* became the original headquarters of the First Wimborne Minster Boy Scouts, but this building also has disappeared. The gateway was preserved, however, and stands at the entrance to the Scouts' present home in Wimborne, in Redcotts Lane, where the Troop's founder is honoured by a commemorative plaque, which reads: "Erected to the memory of 'Doc' Bernard Rayne Parmiter. 'A great Scout'. 19th August 1948". The scene around Leigh Common has changed a great deal in the post-war era; the area where the slaughter-house and the inn and, later, the Scouts hut had stood is now covered by an estate of bungalows, served by roads which, however, at least remember "Doc" Parmiter's name. Across the Common, as already mentioned, modern bungalows have taken the place of the old thatched cottages which once stood there.

On the northern side of the old railway bridge, the road divides, giving the choice of three routes up the hill, Leigh Lane, to the right, Beaucroft Lane, to the left, and Northleigh Lane stright ahead. In 1913, when, of course, most traffic was still horse-drawn, the National Equine League asked permission to erect a "Bearing or home rein" notice at the foot of the hill here. A large hollow, on the right, at the bottom of the hill, once much bigger, marks the site of an old gravel pit, shown on the 1885 Ordnance Survey map.

Northleigh House is halfway up the hill on the left of this road; this large mansion, dating from the early Victorian era, in its own extensive grounds, has been largely restored to something of its former glory through the labours of Stanley and Margaret Walker, who occasionally open the gardens to the public. The house was built for the Wimborne maltster, Charles Webb, whose descendants have reverted to the old Scottish family name and title, Naesmyth of Posso. Webb and his family seem to have lived in the house in an opulent style for several years. He and his wife, Minnie (or Mimi), their two sons and two daughters, and four domestic servants are recorded in the 1891 census, living at Northleigh, and Northleigh Cottage, at the side of the House, was occupied by their gardener, Thomas Hannam. One of the cottages across the road, adjoining the Coach House, was occupied by the groom and coachman, Charles Blandford, and the other by Mrs Webb's parents, the Dublin-born lawyer, John Boulger, and Jemima, of Scots descent. The malting business appears to have fallen on hard times towards the end of the nineteenth century, and the Webbs moved, selling the estate to General Sir John Glyn. Gracious living returned to Northleigh after the Great War, when the estate was purchased by Selwyn Stringer, an industrialist from the Birmingham area. He apparantly made his fortune in the iron and steel business. The local landed gentry, traditionally rather scornful of the "nouveau riche" (and possibly somewhat envious of their ostentatious style of living – there were no fewer than four motor cars owned by the family, at a time when to own just one was sufficient to ensure a place well up the social ladder), dubbed the Stringer family the "Ironmongers". No doubt, they were soon accepted, with their lavish hospitality, as social equals.

Further up the hill from Northleigh House, at the road junction known as the Fiveways, stands the village War Memorial.

Among the names inscribed on it is that of Selwyn Stringer's younger son, Brian. He was a young Lieutenant serving on the battleship, HMS *Barham*, who was lost at sea when the ship was sunk in the Mediterranean by a U-boat in November 1941. The memory of the ill-fated vessel has been perpetuated in the name of the Gorleston-on-Sea lifeboat, the cost of which was partly funded from a substantial bequest in memory of Brian Stringer by his brother, Colin.

At the outbreak of war in 1939, then, the Stringer family was firmly established as one of the leading households in village society, their respectability beyond reproach. The young man, as noted, perished at sea, in the service of his country; and his father, Selwyn, was appointed the chief Air Raid Warden for the village. This background makes a rumour, current at the time, and which has recently been recalled, quite incredible. Rumours, of course, abounded during the war, in the absence of "hard" news imposed by the authorities. One would expect that the navigators in the German bombers flying over the village would have readily pin-pointed their precise position with the aid of the reflections from the glass-houses of the Vineries and the shining metals of the railway alongside, certainly if there was any moonlight, without the need of any further assistance. However, the story went about that there was a light, directed skywards from Northleigh House, whenever enemy aircraft were in the vicinity! Not only that, but wasn't a prominent member of the household – and I must refrain from mentioning her identity, even in quoting from a rumour – born a "Joyce"?; the sister, no less, of William, "Lord Haw-Haw" himself!

Both Leigh Lane and Northleigh Lane betray evidence of having been used as pack-horse tracks more than 300 years ago, being worn down at various points below the level of the adjoining fields. However, neither road shows this so clearly as Beaucroft Lane. Near the foot of the hill, the continual passage of pack-horse traffic on the light sandy soil, together with the eroding effect of the weather, has so worn the lane that the modern road climbs up the hill in a defile 25 feet below the land on each side. There is a story that Mrs Bernarda Lees, widow of the Lancashire cotton mill owner, had the surface artificially lowered still further, in order to protect her privacy at Beaucroft

House from prying eyes of passing peasants on the highway, when she bought the estate. But the pack-horses and the elements have been mainly responsible for the depth of the ravine.

Beaucroft Lane remains a narrow thoroughfare, without footpaths, giving a tunnel-like appearance for much of the year when the foliage of the trees obscures a great deal of the sun's direct light. It is fit – just fit – for motor traffic, but only the most foolhardy of pedestrians, cyclists or horse-riders would venture along this way. However, high alongside the metalled road, runs a gravel track, a service road for the houses built there more than 60 years ago. Harry Langer, the retired Wimborne saddler, and Colehill Parish councillor, lived in one of these properties. This public-spirited man, who lived to be 81, served in the Royal Navy during the 1939-1945 war, sailing in frigates on the convoys to Murmansk, for which he received a medal from the Russians, and he has left his own memorial. It seemed to him that he and his family and neighbours were exposed to death or injury in the event of an air raid during the war – and, indeed, there *were* bombs and machine-gun bullets on Colehill

Beaucroft Lane 1993. The steps leading up to Harry Langer's house can be seen in the right foreground.

on occasions – and conceived the idea of using the hollow-way as a kind of air raid shelter. It was he who cut the steps in the steep slope down to the roadway, which still survive, despite the ravages of the weather, 50 years on, providing them with a hand-rail, to give access from his home to his "shelter". Feeling the steps to be unsafe, as indeed they were latterly, he eventually sealed them off, as the photograph shows. The finger-post, at the top of the steps, pointing to "Rowlands and Colehill" was also provided by Langer, who removed it from the wall of his shop in Wimborne, when he sold the property on his retirement. He found the sign for Ferndown on a rubbish tip, and, deciding that the indicated four miles distance was a reasonably accurate measurement, added this to his sign-post. Langer was a good friend to the Colehill Cricket Club, and younger members were able to buy bats from his shop at a discount; he also rewarded specially good individual performances with a money prize. His uncle, George Langer, chairman, at one time, of the Parish Council, was an architect, specialising in the design of public houses, one of which was the rebuilt *Horns Inn*.

Beaucroft Lane 1993, at the top of the steps outside Langer's house, with the sign giving local directions.

2

Up The Hill

Half-way up the hill, along Beaucroft Lane, where the gravel service road links up again with the sunken road, which has surfaced at this point and is level with the land each side, the big house on the right is Beaucroft House, the focal point a century ago of an estate of about 40 acres. The Beaucroft Estate was purchased from the Hanham family, and the House built by a wealthy widow, a native of Mexico, Mrs Bernarda Lees. She was prominent in village affairs, especially those of the church, in the early years of this century. She died in 1912, but descendants of hers still live at Lytchett Minster. During the Great War, the House was converted into a hospital run by the British Red Cross. Miss E.D. Kemble was Acting Commandant

Beaucroft House 1986.

for three months from December 1914, and Miss Carr Glyn, a member of the illustrious local family, became Commandant – a post equivalent, presumably, in civilian terms, to Matron – for the following four years, until the Hospital closed in April 1919.

Little is known now of the patients there, in their red ties and "Hospital Blue" uniforms, sent straight from the Front in Flanders and France; but at least one of them was a local man, Herbert Habgood, wounded at Ypres, and gassed, while serving with the Durham Light Infantry, who survived to run a building business in the village, following in the same trade as his father, William, builder of the "new" Primitive Methodist Church.

Later incumbents of Beaucroft House were Lt Commander Steer, a retired Naval Officer, and Sir Charles Rugge-Price. Later, the rest of the estate having been sold, the House was divided into three dwellings and survives today in this form. Beaucroft Lodge and the former coach-house (Beaucroft "Mews") remain as further reminders of the former Estate; so, also, does an older property, further down the hill, the Beaucroft Dairy Cottage, once the abode of the civil engineer and historian, Reginald Willcox, and which, earlier, during the Great War, had housed the Beaucroft Laundry, run by Mesdames Christopher, Newman and Alice Dacombe, wife of Alfred, the violinist in the Broomhill Orchestra, to serve the wounded soldiers at the House. The cottage had earlier been the home of Mrs Lees' outdoor staff – the 1891 census shows that the gardener, Frederick Prince, and the groom and coachman, John Parr, lived there. There is no evidence of a brick-kiln in the immediate vicinity, but there is an old clay-pit nearby, and it is said that clay from this source was used for the bricks to build Beaucroft House.

The road forks, Beaucroft Road making a distinct left turn as it climbs the hill, with Beaucroft Lane, now a cul-de-sac (so far as motorists are concerned) continuing straight ahead, and both reach the summit at the highest point in the village – 225 feet above sea level – at Wimborne Road. This main thoroughfare through the village is now a purely residential street, on the southern side, and the houses look out across the road to fields and woods, the rural aspect being interrupted only by

[33]

Henry Farrant, c. 1925, with his Ford lorry outside his garage in Wimborne Road.

the Beaucroft School, built in the old woodland and over the erstwhile Colehill Pond. This started life as the Wimborne Day Special School, and moved up the hill to its newly-built accomodation in 1974, where it was presided over by Peter Butler. Tim Mumford succeeded him as Headmaster in 1978, and continued in office for fourteen years, before handing over to Andrew Mears. Wimborne Road though, 50 years ago, was a fairly busy commercial district, with a carrier's business, and no fewer than four shops, as well as a Police House. Both of the grocer's shops survived into the 1980s.

Henry Farrant, the baker at Leigh Common before the Great War, started his carrier's business here in the 'twenties. The garage for his old Ford lorry still stands. Further along the road, going towards the cricket ground, was the workshop where Charlie Matcham sold and repaired bicycles, having moved from his old premises at the Coffee Tavern. He was brought up – presumably as a foster-child – by the Guy family and had started his business in partnership with Joe Guy, the blacksmith. Matcham is remembered as quite a "character" in the village during the 'twenties and 'thirties. His workshop was a Mecca for all the village lads. Later in life, after the war, he had progressed from pedal cycles to motor bikes, riding one himself, but travelling at so sedate a speed that PC O'Hara, the village constable, mounted on a push-bike, remembers overtaking him. Matcham also became an enthusiastic – almost fanatical – supporter of the Colehill Cricket Club. Next door to Matcham's premises was the Police House. PC Lake was the first resident policeman in the village, and other local "bobbies" associated with the house were Genge, Alf Burridge and Freddy Parsons. Burridge, serving at Colehill during the 1939-45 war, is remembered as "the scourge of the village boys" who would administer "a thick ear" to any he caught "scrumping" apples from Stringer's orchard at Northleigh.

Then came the two grocery shops. The first of them, built in 1864, was a bakery business, owned originally by Cobb. Frank Baldwin bought the business soon after the Great War, and his son, Ted, helped in the shop and drove the pony and trap on an extensive delivery round, before the family aspired to a

Frank Baldwin, c.1925, in his Swift, with a grocery delivery box on the back.

motor van. Behind the saleshop, there was, and is, an extensive range of outbuildings, including the old bakehouse and the old stable, now a garage. Frank gave up the bakery side of the business in 1935, running the shop purely as a grocery, at which time Ted branched out on his own and eventually set up his own bakery business at Farrant's old shop at Leigh Common. Eric Osman worked as an errand boy with Frank, and, as such, became familiar with the big houses in the neighbourhood – Beaucroft, Bells, Onslow, and so on – but with the tradesmen's entrances rather than the grand front doors, and rubbing shoulders, not with the Rugge-Prices, Sollys and Truells, but with their kitchen maids.

Frank Baldwin died in 1941, but the business stayed in the family, his daughter, Winnie Hall, taking over, until selling the shop in 1970, to its last owners, Reg and Delphine Batchelor. Osman kept up his connection with the business, his wife,

Delphine Batchelor's Shop 1980. Delphine, wife of Reg, was the actual owner of the business.

Relics of Baldwin's Shop and Bakery 1994. The old shop-blind, hanging on the door of the garage – earlier the stable.

Betty, working in the shop, and he having a common interest with Batchelor in collecting old agricultural implements. Batchelor's vast collection of souvenirs, a veritable museum, housed in the old bakehouse, includes memorabilia from the shop, which finally shut its doors in 1980, cigarette and match vending machines and enamel signs, and Baldwin's old shop blind, as well as a variety of items, ranging from old petrol cans, at one extreme, to a 1933 Rolls-Royce, at the other. Several trade bicycles, with front baskets, old sparking plugs,

The old bakehouse.

a bulb motor horn, a valve radio (in working order) and a womble, a tool for making straw ropes, are among a host of other items in this private hoard. Batchelor, ex-flight engineer and air gunner in Lancasters and Wellingtons, had the distinction of installing the first computer in Dorset, when he moved to the district from Leamington Spa.

Part of Reg Batchelor's collection 1994. Souvenirs from his wife's shop.

Wimborne Road c. 1919. This is before the days of footpaths and tarmacced roads. Exceptionally keen eyesight is required to decipher the name Brown above the shop. This later became West's shop. Baldwin had not yet arrived in the village. What was later to become his shop is at the extreme left of the picture.

The other grocer's shop closed down at much the same time. It started up before the Great War, in the ownership of H. Burling, who was succeeded by his daughter. Brown was the next to own the shop, and he sold it to Reg Joy, who, in turn, was followed by Reg West. The business continued under a succession of owners, until its demise, caused, as was the case with so many other small shops, by the competition from the super-markets. West, an octogenarian, has recalled in his retirement many anecdotes of village life. One of his customers soon after the second German war was a relative of the Queen, Rev the Hon Andrew Elphinstone, who had come to live at Rowney House, and who was Curate at Wimborne Minster. His order frequently included what he called "dippy" biscuits – presumably to be consumed, American fashion, after "dunking" in tea or coffee.

[40]

Wimborne Road c. 1935. Both grocery shops are visible in this photograph, and the notice in the window of the corner shop, right, at the corner of Beaucroft Lane, advertises a sharpening service for scissors and shears. The road has been surfaced and a footpath provided. The bench on the left, which has been removed within the last few years, bore a plaque in memory of Robert Seymour, the first Highway Surveyor to the Wimborne and Cranborne RDC.

The grocery shops are now private houses, but the other shops have been demolished. One of them stood at the junction of Wimborne Road and Beaucroft Road. Nisbet was the last to occupy it, as a wireless workshop. It had been opened in 1933 by a Mr Low; at one time, it was Mrs White's grocery shop, and it saw service during the latter part of the 1939-45 war as a United States "PX", the American equivalent, roughly, of the British NAAFI. The Colehill Shoe Repair Service occupied the premises during the 'fifties. In the photograph, there is an advertisement for knife and scissor grinding. For a long time, indeed, it was known simply as "the empty shop" – a sad little

Village Outing c. 1945. Among those who have been identified are Gertie Dacombe, Mrs Alice Dacombe, Mrs Winnie Hall, another Mrs Hall, Mrs Dorothy Bryant, Mrs Pitcher and Winnie Pitcher (back row 1st, 2nd, 6th, 7th, 8th, 9th and 10th from left); Burt, the tailor, Harris Winton, who drove the coach, Aileen Burt, David Bryant, and Bert Hall (front row 1st, 4th – behind small boy, John Burt, 5th, 8th, and 9th from left).

piece of private enterprise, which arrived late on the scene, was unloved, apparently, by the local gentry, and was pulled down, unmourned. Another business in this road in the latter part of the nineteenth century was a candle-making factory, at the corner of Beaucroft Lane; and weaving was carried on in a shed, belonging to Mrs Lees, at the corner of Tower Lane and Beaucroft Road: Colehill tweeds had quite a vogue at that time, finding favour in high society, including royalty.

Among the local residents on their coach outing were Harris Winton, who drove the bus, Winnie Hall, David Bryant, who worked in the building trade, served on the Parish Council for some years, and lived to be 85, and his wife, Dorothy (or Dolly), a cook of some considerable reputation, who used to supply pies and other delicacies by arrangement to "the big houses".

The Water Tower was built in 1903 and served the village for more than 80 years before being demolished. There is nothing left now to remind us of its existence apart from the name of the road, Tower Lane, where it stood. The site is now occupied by a small estate of bungalows and their gardens. The story of its origin and how mains water came to be provided to the village over the years is not without interest.

A reservoir, covered to protect the drinking water against pollution, used originally to supply Park Homer House and Beaucroft House, pre-dated the tower which was built along-side. Water was pumped up to the tower, which had a capacity

The Water Tower c. 1910

of nearly 14,000 gallons, from the Walford works during the day, and fed, by gravitation, to the village during the night. The total capacity of the reservoirs and the tower combined was very nearly 179,000 gallons. The reservoir was originally supplied from the old pumping station, beside the River Allen below Walford Bridge, in the fields once belonging to Walford Farm.

This was where the well was sunk, at the bottom of Gundry's fields, from which the Wimborne Minster Waterworks Company pumped water, to supply the town and its reservoir up the hill at Tower Lane. This was some years before the Bournemouth Gas and Water Company moved into the town, to set up its own water works, abstracting water from the Allen higher up the river, above Walford Bridge to supply Bournemouth. The Bournemouth company's waterworks, which still survives, was later connected to the Colehill tower, but the site of the Wimborne company's pumping station, which closed down several years after the arrival of its competitor, following a merger of the firms, is covered now by a housing estate. The two pumping stations, within 600 yards of each other, the one supplying Bournemouth and the other catering for Wimborne and Colehill, co-existed for about twelve years, before merging in 1912. The Colehill reservoir had been empty some years before the demolition of the tower in 1984.

The Water Company's plan of Colehill in the early years of the century shows the extent of its distribution at that time, through 3-inch mains. The entire lengths of Wimborne Road, Giddylake and Greenhill Road were served, with an extension from the latter at *The Horns* to Deans Grove. Eastward extensions connected the Vicarage, Park Homer House, Northleigh House, Leigh Vinery and Beaucroft House. Highland Road, for some reason, seems to have been favoured with a 4-inch main.

The wrought-iron gate into the cricket field commemorates the service rendered to Colehill Cricket Club over many years, as player and administrator, by Archie Guy. His father and grandfather had, in their day, both been stalwarts of the Club. Joseph Hardy Guy, the grandfather, had, indeed, been a founder member of the club, Colehill St Michael's, as it was

Archie Guy Memorial Gate at Colehill Cricket Ground 1993.
The Solly family oaks line the boundary beyond.

[45]

then known, back in 1905. He was the village blacksmith until taking over Colehill Farm. Meanwhile, his son, Joseph Edward, had succeeded him in the smithy, and had continued the Guy cricketing tradition. Archie, whose memorial stands within hailing distance of the old water tower site, was, in fact, employed at the water works at Walford.

The aerial photograph of the old Bells Estate, taken in the early 'fifties, embraces much else of Colehill, looking in a south-easterly direction. The old railway line is in the far distance, running across the top centre and right of the picture, with what looks very much like a steam train setting out from Wimborne Station. Beaucroft Lane can be seen, running off to the top, from the rather prominent triangle of roads, to the

The Bells Estate c. 1950.

[46]

left. Wimborne Road runs across the centre of the picture, from left to right, forming one side of this triangle (which, perhaps, is the neighbourhood at the top of Rowlands known 60 years ago as "The Island"). The two parallel roads curving round from Wimborne Road to Beaucroft Lane are Highland Road, and, nearer the camera, Tower Lane. The water tower is visible, although partly obscured by a tree, and, beside it, one (and perhaps two) of the reservoirs which watered the village. Giddylake starts almost in the centre of the photograph, and disappears at the bottom right. Onslow House, where Robert Truell and his family lived a century ago, is just to the right of this track, and Bells House, home of the Solly family, to the left. Both houses have been converted into flats. The old coach house of Bells, where Solly's horses (and, later, his motor car) lived downstairs, and his coachman, Ernest Way, with his family, lived upstairs, has been converted into an attractive residence called High Hanger (previously known as Puffins), and is a little further to the left. The road running off to the left centre of the picture is Greenhill Close, at the end of which two of the other big houses, Wingreen and St. Audrey's, are visible.

The extensive Bells Estate reached as far as Wimborne Road, and included the cricket ground – the large field adjoining the road. The Cricket Club has had its home here since 1923, sharing it at first with the farmer, Johnny Coakes, as co-tenants of the Sollys. The Club purchased the ground when the Bells Estate was sold, more than 40 years ago, although ownership of the splendid oak trees at the northern end of the ground was retained, and still is, by the Solly family. Some very good cricketers have graced this field on behalf of the Club down the years, a few of whom, indeed, have gone on to represent Dorset; Richard Scott rose to even dizzier heights, playing first-class cricket for Hampshire and Gloucestershire. A large part of the village life has been centred here, and many of the well-known men and boys of the village have been prominent in the club: the three generations of Guys; three generations of Scotts, from Reg, his son, Andy, down to Richard and his brothers; Reg Welch, and his sons, Jim and John; Henry Habgood, and his son, Ralph: these and others illustrious in its annals have

Onslow House c. 1989.

ensured that the Colehill Cricket Club has achieved much success, both on the field of play, in competition with the leading club sides in Dorset, and, in a social sense, within the village itself. Many will recall, for example, the annual festivities on 5 November, and the superb display of fireworks, and the great bonfires (sited well away from the sacred "square").

Rowlands Hill, named after an adjoining field of some antiquity (and, no doubt, its owner of the time), is the continuation of Wimborne Road as it drops down into the town. It was earlier known as Bullpits Road, from the hollow in the grounds of Glen House, which has been described as a bull pit, or, alternatively, as a bear pit. A street plan of Wimborne, dated 1775, shows the Bullpitt, then owned by Sir William Hanham. Bell Lane seems to have been an even earlier name for the road, as the Woodward Survey of 1775, marking the boundary of the Bankes and Hanham Estates, shows it thus. A legal document of the same date, delimitating the boundary between the Estates hereabouts, gives Bells Lane and Colehill Lane as further alternatives. Bells House clearly takes its name from the Lane and the large meadows running from it down to the River Allen, Bells, Great Bells and the Ringing Ground, then part of Walford Farm, owned by Gundry, presumably that same Nathaniel Gundry who still owned the vast Uddens Estate at that time, whereas Onslow House was named after its first owner, the Rev C. Onslow, whose daughter married General Truell.

Remains of Cobb's brick kiln c. 1989.

3
Over The Hill

The scene remains quite rural as one descends the hill on the far side, and our ancestors of a century ago would find most of it fairly familiar.

The remains of the old brick-kiln where John William Cobb and his descendants and their men fired their bricks and agricultural pipes for a hundred years before the Great War, and the large pit where they dug their clay, can still be discerned

Brickyard Farm c. 1990.

Brickyard Cottage 1992.

in the yard of Brickyard Farm. And, another 75 years on, the scene appears to be ready to change again, following the death of Frank Peckham, who kept his cattle here. Indeed, his home for much of his life, the old thatched cottage in Burts Hill, just below *The Horns*, has already been demolished, and its place taken by a substantial brick-built house. Among Peckham's effects, auctioned after his death, were some rare, vintage items, such as an old peck measure. An acetylene headlamp for his ancient motor-cycle was also in the sale.

Above the clay-pit, Brickyard Cottage, once the home of one of Cobb's workers, still watches over the changed scene. Louisa Butler, in her 90th year, had memories from her childhood, when she lived in the cottage, of seeing the glow from the brick-kiln at nighttime. The address on her marriage certificate, in 1929, is given as "Brickyards, Greenhill". She was the daughter of Henry Frampton, a journeyman brickmaker, who was the last of the brickmakers, and became the first of the farmers on the site. Henry and his wife, Mary, adopted or fostered the young Frank Peckham, who eventually became the natural successor to the farm.

Above the brick works, a timber merchant, Bailey, had a saw-mill, and, nearby, Thomas Major and Son had a builders' yard, at the Greenhill Works, to complete an industrial scene difficult to imagine today. Major's son, Charlie, who married Winifred Pank, a teacher at Middlehill School, continued the business, eventually selling it to Albert White. Burt, the village tailor, had his business at Greenhill, before selling it to Randall, and emigrating to New Zealand.

At the foot of Greenhill Road, where it joins Burts Hill, stands *The Horns Inn*, a hostelry of considerable antiquity. *The Horns Ale House*, which, together with the garden and adjoining plot, covered more than two acres – just as it does today – was owned by the Bankes Estate, and leased to John Barnes at the time of the Woodward Survey of 1775 and, no doubt, its origins go back even earlier. Charles Harding was the licensee in 1851, and had been succeeded by Samuel Smith 20 years later. His widow, Mary, is shown as inn-keeper in the 1891 Census. The old picturesque, thatched building was destroyed in a fire in 1929, and there was a proposal that Charles Ellis, the Wimborne brewer who owned the property, should build a private house for himself on the site. This failed to materialise, however, and eventually the inn was rebuilt, as we know it today. Ellis Brothers sold the inn, together with several others in the district, including *The Barley Mow*, to the Blandford brewers, Hall and Woodhouse, in 1935. Capt F.A. Worley, an ex-Royal Artillery officer, held the license at that time, when the hostelry was advertising "luncheons, camping, swings and tea gardens". Worley was followed by a retired naval man, Lieut Comm C. Heathcote, and then M.B. Linds. An unhappy period in the early 'fifties followed, when much of the local custom left and the local policeman was obliged to give warnings about after-hours drinking. Order was restored when Walter Churchill took over the license, and he was succeeded, in the late 'sixties, by Bob Wrigley. The present incumbents, Ivor and Rose Thomas, took over in 1972.

It is clear from the Woodward Survey that at that time most of the land on the south side of Burts Hill down towards Walford was already under cultivation, with nurseries and market gardens being recorded. Some of the land adjoining Burts Hill to its north belonged to the Hanham family, but to its Manor of Wilksworth rather than its Deanery Estate. The land runs away down towards Dogdean and Furzehill; the old names for trackways here, Batchelors Drong, Doll Davy Lane and so on, are long gone and forgotten, like the people whose names they bore. "Drong" is an old Dorset name for a narrow track. The intersection of Doll Davy Lane – known today as Dogdean – and the Cranborne road was called Minstrels Cross in 1775; and Dogdean Common was known as Bellfurze.

The Gaunts Estate, owned by the Glyns, subsequently acquired Deans Grove (which itself, somewhat confusingly, was originally known as Dogdean), the tenant of which was John Hatchard, born in 1809, who farmed a considerable acreage in the district, as much as 500 acres at the time of the 1881 census, when he employed sixteen men and four boys, and who

Deans Grove 1987, immediately before the arrival of Dumpton School.

[54]

was succeeded by William Coakes, and, later, by *his* son, John. The house became the home, during the early years of this century, of Charles Hay, a leading luminary and sportsman in the village, and brother-in-law of its first Vicar, Cyril Kindersley. The property was later sold to Morley and from him it passed into commercial ownership, first by Christopher Hill, and then by Rank Hovis MacDougall. The seventeenth century mansion now houses the Dumpton School, which purchased the property and the extensive grounds in 1987. The school took its name from its original home when founded in 1903, Dumpton House, near Broadstairs, Kent. War-time evacuation caused a move to Crichel House in 1939, and it has stayed in Dorset ever since. The school became tenants of the Glyn Estate when it moved to Gaunts House in 1946, and it was during its sojourn there that the present headmaster, Garth Watson, was appointed, in 1978.

The isolated building standing back from Burts Hill, down from *The Horns*, away from Wimborne, is Chapel Cottage, the first Christian place of worship on Colehill. This is where Hawke and Parsons, and their fellow dissenters from

Burts Hill, at the foot of Greenhill c. 1990. The building is Chapel Cottage; the inn-sign belongs to The Horns.

Wimborne, ostracised from the town, congregated, and thus set up the first Methodist Church in the village. They were eventually to build their own mud-built chapel, and then the present church, both in Lonnen Road, but the Methodists continued to use Chapel Cottage until the early years of this century. Chapel Cottage appears to be on the site of the property leased to Samuel Burden "with the Brick Kiln" at the time of the Woodward Survey. Indeed, it is very probably the *same* building, as a pit just behind the cottage is very suggestive of clay extraction. On the other hand, this pit is marked on the 1885 Ordnance Survey map as a gravel pit, and, assuming that this is correct, one still does not need to look further afield to find Burden's brick kiln than the brick works which later belonged to Coombes, just down the hill from St Michael's Church, beside Smugglers Lane (for which "Brick Hill" was a more familiar name three or four generations ago).

The Woodward Survey is a mine of information about the land belonging to the Kingston Lacy Estate and its neighbours, its use and its tenants. The schedule lists all the leaseholders and several names from that eighteenth-century document are still familiar on Colehill today, and are, no doubt, related. The Cole family, for example, is particularly well represented: Edward, John Hayward and Robert, all of that ilk, had leases of land between Burts Hill and Giddylake; and James held more than an acre of arable land and a cottage adjoining "on the top of Colehill adjoining Enclosure from Mr Bankes's Waste" – this would correspond more or less with the present day location of the Cricket Ground.

The plan, accompanying the survey, is a little difficult to read, both on account of the alignment, "north" being toward the bottom right-hand corner of the sheet, and also as some of the trackways marked on it – Middle Bound Way and Studicks Hill Road are two – have now vanished. But the Close "near *The Horns* at Colehill" – more than an acre of arable land – leased to Widow Spencer can be identified with certainty, lying half-way along the track from Chapel Cottage to St Michael's. Elizabeth Osman was the last tenant of the cottage there, known as Mount Pleasant, which was demolished soon after she died, in her mid-nineties, 20 years ago.

Burts Hill, and its continuation, Long Lane, is a very ancient thoroughfare, and lead, down to the far side of the hill, to Long Lane Farm and *The Barley Mow*. The farm, and its neighbour, Colehill Farm, in Colehill Lane, were both held on lease from the Kingston Lacy Estate, and were, indeed, amalgamated when William Oakley Burgess retired. Neither, alas, has survived as a farm, following the death of Henry Bankes in 1981 and the transfer of the whole of the Kingston Lacy Estate to the

Five generations of the Parfitt family c. 1920. In front, on the right, is Ann (known as Granny Bloomer), then aged about 96. Her daughter-in-law is on the left. Her son, Edward, is standing next to his daughter, Annie, who had become Mrs Bugler, and the baby in her arms is his granddaughter, Phyllis.

National Trust the following year. Only Pilford and the small Leigh and Brickyard Farms remain of the many farms and smallholdings which flourished across Colehill a hundred years ago.

Two of the village "characters", well remembered by the older generation, lived near Long Lane Farm. A sub-tenant of

Ann Parfitt c. 1920.

[58]

Burgess, who lived next to the farm, is remembered as something of a recluse, and given to such eccentricities as using a brown paper bag as an item of headgear! This was Sidney Cox, whose family had lived in the cottage since the middle of the nineteenth century. Ann Squibb, no doubt related to the family

421 Merryfield c. 1935. This was the Parfitt home for generations. Ann lived here after her marriage, her grandson, Edward, lived here all his life, and his granddaughter, Phyllis, was born here. The cottage belonged to the Bankes family, but has now been demolished.

Compton-Hall, with his donkey. He was one of the village "characters", and was known familiarly as "Crump". He was a neighbour of the Parfitts, and lived in the end part of their cottage.

of that name who worked some of the gravel pits in the village, married a sawyer, James Parfitt, but was widowed twelve years later. Known familiarly as "Granny Bloomer" throughout the village, Ann Parfitt lived at Merryfield, near its junction with Long Lane, but her old cottage, owned by the Kingston Lacy Estate, was demolished many years ago, after her death. She invariably carried a long stick: this was used, so it was said, to administer summary punishment to children who misbehaved. However, its real purpose seems to have been to shake the pine needles from the trees; these became a valuable fuel – known as "scroth" – to the impoverished. The extreme opulence of the few was matched by the abject poverty of others of her generation. It is difficult for us, in our comparatively affluent society, with the Welfare State supporting the needy, to imagine how hard life was for the poor a century ago. Described as a pauper in the census of 1871, Mrs Parfitt had been a widow since 1860 and had provided for a family of six children. She is said to have worked all day as a farm labourer for tenpence – that is, in today's money, just over fourpence – a day. At another time, she made flannel shirts, working by candlelight at home, and *walked* the nine or ten miles to Poole – and the same distance back – to deliver the finished garments. She earned tenpence for each shirt she made, and subsisted on this, plus half a crown (12½p) "parish" money per week. She died in 1920, nearly 97 years of age. A happier "rags to riches" story records that a grand-son ran away to sea at the age of fifteen and eventually retired with the rank of Lieutenant-Commander! No doubt, many still living in the village can trace their ancestry back to James and Ann Parfitt; others who can definitely do so have moved away and settled in distant parts such as Bridport, in West Dorset, and even as far away as Pinner, in Middlesex.

Nell Shiner lived to a great age – she was more than 80 when she died over 60 years ago – in an isolated cottage in the fields between Long Lane and Colehill Lane. She was well known locally as a dressmaker, although, under pressure, apt to make simple mistakes in her work. She had made, for example, a wedding dress for Kate Elizabeth Budden, but with one cream sleeve and the other white! The cottage, like its occupant, has long since gone: it was never supplied with water, even well water, and neighbours can remember the poor old woman having to climb the hill to fetch water from the nearest well, at Roberts' farm.

Other anecdotes of hard times at the turn of the century, handed down from an earlier generation, abound. Bill Cole's father, Arthur, a brick-layer, who married Kate Budden, had to limp to work at Verwood and back every day – one leg was six inches shorter than the other – taking his lunch, a bottle of cold tea and some bread and cheese, with him. Dorcas Cobb, granddaughter of the brickmaker – who was to marry into one of the branches of the Habgood family and lived to be 96 – could remember schoolchildren of her time taking pitchers to Middlehill School; these were used to collect soup from the kitchen of Park Homer House, on their way home. Mrs Georgiana Paget, at Park Homer, in return for a proper show of respect from the "peasants", seems, like her late husband, to have been of a philanthropic nature, and her charitable works included the provision of soup for out-of-work villagers.

Like *The Horns, The Barley Mow* has a long history, and was

The Barley Mow, Colehill.

Ann Stanger

The Barley Mow, c. 1960, sketched by Ann Stanger.

one of the inns transferred from Ellis Brothers to Hall and Woodhouse, in 1935. At that time, it had only a "Beer On" license, held by its tenant since 1932, John Loveridge (who also had a dairy round). Zilpah Gwendoline Loveridge was the last of several members of that family to hold the license, in 1959, when a full license was granted; she married Edgar Dacombe and survived him, and the license passed from her to Jack Smith.

Local folk-lore has it that the original part of the building was a drover's cottage in the fourteenth century, and that, three centuries later, troops under the command of Cromwell – or Fairfax – were quartered in the neighbourhood. God's Blessing Green and Lane, not far away, are named, so the story goes, from being the site where the protection of the Almighty was sought before they set out to do battle, possibly at Corfe Castle.

The first census – in 1841 – records Reubin Hopkins as the publican; ten years later, Thomas West, native of the Cape of Good Hope, was the licensee. George Ivamy is listed in 1861 as "Grocer, beerseller and farmer of 30 acres", but in 1871, his wife (and perhaps widow – there is no record of George), Jane, was the innkeeper. We come across a widow, Jane Ivamy, again, incidentally, 20 years later – her age tallies and it seems likely to be the same person – when she was listed as "Caretaker of Uddens House", presumably at a time when the mansion was not occupied. The Greatheds, who owned the house, had given up living there and were in the habit of letting it to wealthy gentry.

Meanwhile, at *The Barley Mow*, Joseph Long had taken over by 1881. The Electoral Register for 1886 lists Jesse Puttock as the innkeeper, and a faded photograph from the early years of this century shows the licensee to have been named Steel, with a group of his customers, pint pots in hand, gathered round the door of the old thatched inn, a donkey, and, in the centre of the group, presumably Steel himself, and his lady. One of the regular customers at *The Barley Mow* was Charlie Harding, the local "vet", employed to castrate pigs and other farm animals. The story goes – and it is a familiar one in the folk-lore of many village communities – that he would be carried home, drunk and lying prostrate in his cart, his enterprising horse taking the initiative. On arrival home, Mrs Harding would unhitch the horse and tip her husband out of the cart.

Beyond *The Barley Mow* lies the little hamlet of Broomhill. Broomhill has its own Methodist Church – they were

William Joseph Habgood, c.1930, double-bass player in the Broomhill orchestra.

Wesleyans, as opposed to the Primitives, up the hill – and the music for their services was provided by a String Orchestra, just the sort of church musicians as those described in the novels of Thomas Hardy. The band acquired a considerable reputation, certainly locally, and was much in demand to play at village concerts, as well as playing in the Broomhill chapel. It continued to accompany the singing there until the late 1940s when, at last, even Broomhill changed to the all-conquering church organ. Colehill, though, had, in many ways, claimed the musicians for itself, and, indeed, it was known familiarly as the Colehill String Orchestra. Prominent among its members were village tradesmen such as the carter, Henry Habgood, Joe Guy, blacksmith and farmer, his blacksmith son, "young" Joe, another son, Frank, a daughter, Henrietta (who became Mrs Henry Habgood) and three grandsons, Ted Guy, Frank Habgood and Reg Welch.

Alf Dacombe and his grandson, the future village postmaster, John, c. 1950.

Alf Dacombe, a plasterer by trade, was another prominent member. He played the violin with the band throughout its life, which spanned close on 60 years, and was its leader during its hey-day, in the 'twenties. Sometimes he played in a duo or solo, and stories are told of how, after a day's work – and the hours were long at that time – he would cycle, with his fiddle on his back, more than 30 miles to Weymouth, play at a dance there, and cycle the 30 miles back to Colehill, snatch a few hours' sleep, before starting his labours the next day, perhaps as far away as Crichel, at seven in the morning. He is photographed, about 1950, with his grand-son, John – now the village postmaster – on his knee. Charlie Matcham, the bicycle seller and repairer, who had a fine singing voice, was an occasional performer with the band. Reg Welch became the organist at the church when the band was replaced and retired in 1965 after sharing in the music of the church for 32 years.

Ralph Habgood, Henry's son, wrote an admirable booklet to commemorate the centenary of the Broomhill Church in 1986 – aptly entitled "100 Not Out": the author was a prominent member, indeed secretary for many years, of the Colehill Cricket Club – in which it is clear that many leading Colehill families worshipped at that church beyond the hill. The Methodists had fragmented into three separate organisations, and the rift was not healed until an act of union in the early 1930s. The Wesleyans clearly held different tenets from the Primitives, but there was also, at a time when such things were more important than they are nowadays, a clear social distinction. As the Anglican Church tended to attract the aristocracy and the professional classes, so the Wesleyan Methodists drew their support largely from tradesmen and craftsmen, while the lower echelons of society tended towards the Primitives. This, no doubt, explains, in part, at least, why so many prominent Colehill families attended a church a mile away at Broomhill. Habgood's account of Broomhill includes the amusing tale of another of the village characters, Johnny Gallop, outspoken and perhaps hard of hearing, but, at least, attentive: he is alleged to have shouted to a preacher during a sermon: "Spake up, maister; everybody cain't have front sates"! Habgood, known to many in the village as "Mr Broomhill", continues to be a pillar of strength to the church, as he has been over many years; and, in his book, records the names of others who have been prominent in the first hundred years of its life. Apart from the musicians, already mentioned, these include William Mackrell, Reuben Hayward and Charles Stout.

Pilford Farm, the only sizable survivor of the rich local agricultural tradition in the village, lies across the road from *The*

Elsie and Kit Burden on their pony and trap milk round c. 1930. Middlehill Road is a gravel track, without a footpath. Holmsley Cottages are on the right, with, beyond, the Post Office.

Barley Mow and the Broomhill Church, some short distance back from the eastern side of Colehill Lane, with its approach track running from Pilford Lane. The farm was on part of the once extensive Uddens Estate, until that was broken up and largely sold, more than 20 years ago. Austen Dean became the tenant in 1955 and purchased the freehold in 1974. The farm, of 250 acres, extends beyond Pilford Lane and is almost totally pastoral, the only crop grown being maize to feed its own dairy herd. Another 170 acres were added when the adjoining Bedborough Farm, also part of the Uddens Estate, was purchased in 1988. Dean's predecessor at Pilford was Antell, but its previous history is difficult to trace. The name of Taylor has been mentioned as the tenant of the farm at one time, and Tom Chissell, of Cowgrove Farm, has some recollection that his grandfather, another Tom Chissell, who died in 1923, farmed there.

The road, climbing the hill, to the centre of the village from Broomhill, Colehill Lane, passes the now defunct Colehill Farm, leased from the Kingston Lacy Estate successively by Joseph Hardy Guy when his son, "young" Joe, took over the smithy, Tom Roberts, then *his* sons, Harold and Claude, and finally, Claude's son-in-law, Derek Pope. The farm was leased jointly with that in Long Lane in its last years, closing when the last of the Bankes family to own the Estate died and bequeathed it to the National Trust. Next to the farm, 60 years ago, Arthur Ernest Burden ran the Little Lonnen Dairy, and his daughters, Elsie and Kit, delivered the milk by pony cart to the villagers. Older generations knew this part, where Little Lonnen runs off to the left from Colehill Lane, as "Top o' Cross".

To the east, Pilford, the district between the farm of that name and Glynville, continues to be served by its own little grocery store, The Handy Store, in Lonnen Road, which has managed to survive into the 1990s in the ownership of Mrs Audrey Jupe, descendant of one of the old village families. The modern brick-built shop stands on the site of the old timber building where Mrs Edith White served her customers many years before the war, so the business has a considerable history.

A large area of heathland, Pilford Heath, scarred by numerous gravel pits, once stretched from Lonnen Road, below Glynville, over to Cannon Hill. However much one might deplore the advancing tide of bricks and mortar across what is left of the rural part of the village, the building of the "Bird Sanctuary" estate of houses and bungalows, in the late 'sixties, does not seem to have spoiled much of value. This, of course, is a matter of opinion, but one recalls the bleak scene here one dismal, grey, wintry day in 1962, with the plots for the embryo houses pegged out across the barren land.

4
Middle Hill

Between the years 1896, when Colehill was given its own identity as a Civil Parish, and 1913, when a curious anomaly was rectified, the whole of the eastern part of the village, conforming to the land owned by the Greatheds of Uddens, lay in the civil parish of Hampreston. Hence, the surprising information in the entry for Colehill in Kelly's Directories (for 1903, for example) that the village children "attend the schools at Wimborne and Middle Hill, Hampreston".

Uddens Farm was "To Let", according to an advertisement in the Salisbury Journal in October 1768; and, in July 1786, the Sherborne Mercury advertised: "For sale: Estate and modern-built mansion-house at Uddens. Apply to Nathaniel Gundry esquire". Gundry, the son of a judge, was a great

Middle Hill School c. 1890.

Colehill County First School c. 1990. The original building remains, but the scene is transformed.

MIDDLE HILL SCHOOL 1890. The Headmistress, Elizabeth Chaston, is at the back, on the right. Her daughters, Amy (or Ann) – top – and Clara (or Charlotte) – bottom – are the teachers on the left.

[70]

Middlehill School c. 1921. Front row, l. to r.: Charlie Bullen, Jenkins, Bob Morton, Len Baker, Fred Richmond; second row, l. to r.: Albert Moody, Ken Hall, Cecil Frampton, ?, Les Cullen, ?; third row, l. to r.: Maurice Baker, Vera Newman, Lily Cole, Beryl Shiner, Winnie Richmond, Vera Richmond, Elsie Shearing; back row, l. to r.: Eddie Clarke, Ethel Newman, Winnie Cole, Jessie King, Dorothy Carr, Winnie Hillier, Charlie Sawtell.

land-owner in the district, and, in 1790, he leased the Uddens Estate to the Lincolnshire gentleman, Edward Greathed, who subsequently bought the freehold. It appears that Gundry left Uddens as a result of a new plantation being ridden over by the hunt. Later generations of Greatheds tended to live at, not Uddens House, which would be let to a series of wealthy and, often, aristocratic tenants, but at neighbouring Bedborough. Uddens House, still belonging to the family, was demolished in the mid-1950s, having stood for two centuries.

The Greatheds built the school, Middle Hill School, in 1865, on their Uddens Estate and Mary, niece of the first of the Uddens Greatheds, and mother of the illustrious General Sir Edward Greathed, of Indian Mutiny fame, endowed the foundation. The interest from this investment is still applied for the use of the school despite the attempt of the Dorset County Council to appropriate it a few months after they took over the school in 1935. The original building still stands, surmounted by its now bell-less belfry, and is the oldest surviving public building in the village. It has been much added to in the past 40 years as the school's population has grown, following the vast expansion of the village in the second half of the twentieth century. Additional classrooms have had to be built in part of the school playground and across the road on what was once its extensive sports field, now, alas, sadly diminished. This new playing field replaced a much earlier one, across the road, and adjoining the school, and was laid out in 1961 on the site of one of the many gravel pits, running from here down to Pilford Heath. Like much of Colehill, extensive residential "development" in the past few years has now swallowed up many of the old gravel workings and the rather bleak heathland down towards Pilford.

Middlehill School c. 1921. Front row: Stan Hebditch (centre); second row, l.to r.: Winnie Burden, Winnie Cole, Winnie Richmond, Kathy Hebditch, Beryl Shiner, Vera Newman, Vera Richmond; third row, l. to r.: Dollie Hillier, Dolly White, Flossie Shearing, Kitty Burden, Jessie King, Dorothy Carr, Gwen Hall; back row, l. to r.: Herbert Cullen, ?, ?, Eddie Clarke, ?, ?, ?, Charles Lodge (the Headmaster).

Middlehill School c. 1921. Front row, l. to r.: Alec Moore, Alfred Moore, Ken Shiner, Bob Hayward, Eric Habgood, George Thorne; middle row, l. to r.: Shearing, Cyril Cole, Harold Habgood, ?, David Cobb, Stan Sawtell, ?; back row, l. to r.: Wareham, Arthur Moore, ?, Fred Poore, Eric Gollop, Walter Jenkins, ?, ?.

Middlehill School c. 1925.

The old Schoolhouse adjoined the school, and successive Headmistresses and Headmasters, from the first, Elizabeth Chaston, with her daughters, Charlotte and Ann (or Amy), both of whom later assisted in the school as pupil teachers, in 1865, down to Charles Lodge in the 1920s, lived there. In those days, when, of course, travelling, especially in rural areas, was far from easy, Head Teachers tended to live "over the shop", but the modern tendency seems to be for them to live as far as possible from their schools – and from complaining parents! One, indeed, lives 20 miles away, over the Hampshire border.

Val Griffith was very active in village affairs, when he succeeded Lodge, in the mid-twenties. His interests included the church and the Boy Scouts, of which he was the first Scoutmaster when the local troop was formed. Above all, he is

MIDDLEHILL SCHOOL c. 1921. Front row, l. to r.: ?, Maurice Moody, ?, ?, Gilbert Richmond, ?; middle row: ?, Thorn, Hayward, Nellie Thorne, Jessie Hall, Ethel Coombs, Herbert Cullen, Ron Brewer; back row: Charles Lodge (Headmaster) with Gerald Hall in his arms, Frank Middleton, Stanley Habgood, ?, Ken Shiner, Ralph Hall, Jim Guest, ?.

fondly remembered by his old pupils for his great interest in choral music. Indeed, in this sphere also, his influence extended beyond the school, into village life, as he was the conductor of the Women's Institute Choir. After four years, Griffith moved to pastures new. His successor as Headmaster of Middlehill School was R. Charlton, who stayed for less than two terms. He was followed by W.A. Greenland, another devotee of music, and remembered with much affection.

The School "Log" for the years 1899 to 1955 is still extant, although that for the early years of the school, which must have

Middlehill School Choir c.1933. Front row, l. to r.: Marjorie Cole, Jim Frampton, Betty Smith, Kathy Hillyer, Gladys Portsmouth, Leah Baker, Gladys Baker, Barbara Shepherd, Ethel Coombs, Betty Shiner; second row, l. to r.: Marjorie Willis, Mabel Thorne, May Allen, ?, Margaret Freeman, Molly Habgood, ?, Brenda Habgood, Eva Hall, Vera Frampton; third row, l. to r.: Alan Jones, ?, Arthur James, Phil Baker, Ralph Hall, Jim Guest, Ron Richmond,?, Ron Fiander; in the back row, Maurice Moody is second from the left; W.A.Greenland, the Headmaster, stands on the left, and Winifred Pank, a teacher, who later married the builder, Charlie Major, stands on the right.

Middlehill School Pantomime 1933. "Sinbad the Sailor". Les Hall is on the extreme right of the front row; back row, l. to r.: Ron Fiander, Bert Selby, Eva Hall, Brenda Habgood, Richard Hinton (a master), Marjorie Cole, W.A.Greenland (Headmaster), Jim Guest, Bob Freeman, Ron Richmond, ?.

been fascinating reading, has disappeared. However, the record for the first half of this century holds up an interesting mirror to the life, not only of the school, but outside, as well, reflecting social and other aspects of the village. Mary Hart succeeded Elizabeth Chaston, who had been Headmistress of the school for its first 34 years, in 1899. In November of that year, she had to record: "... a very poor attendance today, about 15 boys stopping away beating for the shooters". The local gentry clearly had first claim to the scholars' time. The school had a half holiday on 21 May 1900, to celebrate the Relief of Mafeking. Miss Hart had become Mrs Martin, and was succeeded as Head by Sarah Tapley in 1901.

Other school holidays resulted from the Band of Hope "treat", the "Little *Lonen* Sunday School treat", the Proclamation of Peace, after the Boer War, in June 1902 and such other national or local festive occasions. Allegiances to a variety of local Christian organisations – the Broomhill Methodists, the

Congregationalists, the Roman Catholics, the Baptists, the "Trinity" Chapel, the Rechabites and even the Hampreston Anglicans – who arranged treats and outings ensured further holidays: such absences were sanctioned for those qualified to attend. How many children, one wonders, belonged to more than one church? The children had a week's holiday to celebrate the coronation of Edward VII. On another occasion, the school had to close because of the illness of all the teachers.

The "log" records the names of new pupils, and it is of interest to note the names of little boys of five or six who were to live to a great age and become prominent figures in village life in manhood. In the month of April 1902, for example, William Cole and David Bryant were among the new boys. A note of some personal anguish is struck in an entry in July 1915, presumably by Lodge himself: "The master's teeth (last few) being extracted to enable him to be right by end of the holiday". The summer holidays, known at that time as the Harvest Holiday – an indication of how rural the community then was – did not begin before the end of July. The dire shortage of food towards the end of the Great War is reflected in two half-holidays being granted for blackberry picking "for the food controller". Nearly one cwt. were weighed each afternoon. One child was diagnosed as having a weak heart and was "not to be even scolded should she be a naughty girl": license surely for any amount of mischief!

Considerable controversy seems to have arisen in the village when the education authorities ordained that girls over eleven should be transferred to the Wimborne Minster Girls' School, after Easter 1934. This unpopular move was resisted, and the girls, supported by a group of parents, turned up at Middlehill on the first day of the new term, demanding entry. This was refused, but the dispute appears to have lasted throughout the summer term, and involved a petition to the County Council by the parents. The bureaucrats eventually prevailed and the protest fizzled out. Having spent the first 70 years of its life as the Greathed Charity School, Middlehill became a Council School in 1935, and was designated an Infant and Junior School when it reopened for the autumn term. The fondly remembered Greenland resigned in 1936 and Florence

Trenaman was appointed as the new Head. She served in this capacity for the next 19 years, until she was succeeded by Miss Mildred Gillett, who was in charge at the time of the great population explosion of both the village and the school in the 'sixties. Ray Wardle was the next Head and he was succeeded by Valerie Cox, now Mrs Marshall.

The old schoolhouse was extended to form Quarry Corner, otherwise known as Quarry Bottom, one of the large houses of the area, in the early 1920s by its new owner, Lieut-Colonel the Hon Alfred Frederick William Harris. He was the younger brother of the fifth Earl of Malmesbury, of Hurn Court, whose large estate embraced the whole of Hurn and much of the north-eastern part of Bournemouth. The Colonel, whose wife was Margaret Elizabeth, sister of the eleventh Baron Belhaven and Stenton, made his home at Quarry Corner for about 20 years, following his retirement after a distinguished military career, both in South Africa, when he served at the siege of Ladysmith, before being wounded, and in the Great War, when he held the rank of Major, was Mentioned in Dispatches and was again wounded. Harris became active in village affairs, especially in connection with the school. Mrs Winifred Lethbridge, second daughter of the Broomhill violinist, Alfred Dacombe, was in service at Quarry Corner, successively as housemaid, parlourmaid and cook, in its early years, before leaving to be married. She treasures fond memories of her employers, especially an incident when Harris entertained some guests at a dinner party. Among them was Helen Armstrong, better known as the celebrated Australian soprano Dame Nellie Melba. Mrs Lethbridge was specially sent for, to be congratulated on her cooking by Dame Nellie in person. As a girl, Winifred Dacombe had attended the adjoining Middlehill School, walking there from her home with the Loveridge sisters from *The Barley Mow*, and remembers the oil lamps by which the school was lighted. She also recalls from those days of the Great War the employment of German prisoners for the felling and lopping of fir trees.

Quarry Corner later became the home of "Taffy" Howell-Evans and his wife. Pat O'Hara recalled one incident in the early 'fifties concerning this couple, when he, as the village

George Squibb and his wife c. 1948.

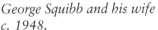
Bertie Squibb c. 1948.

policeman, was entrusted by Mrs Howell-Evans with £20, to be distributed among the children at the School. She was so pleased with the improved conduct of the children, following O'Hara's arrival at the new Police House, not very far away in Middlehill Road, that she felt that they should be rewarded. £20, divided by 160, the number of pupils, provided half-a-crown for each child, and O'Hara lined up the scholars, and dispensed the bounty accordingly. Alas, for such neat arithmetic, there proved to be a total, in fact, of 161 pupils, and the policeman found himself, at the end of the line, and the money all gone, with one more small rather dejected boy. There was a happy ending to this story, although O'Hara found himself half-a-crown out of pocket at the end of the exercise!

Quarry Corner was demolished in the mid-sixties to make room for a modest estate of new dwellings. The house had taken its name from the extensive gravel workings, worked for Elizabeth Oldfield, of the Uddens Estate, by the Squibb family, George and his sons, Bert, Harry and Arthur. The gravel was carried away by horse and cart by the haulier, Ernie Hoare.

Two other substantial properties in the vicinity, both belonging to the second half of the nineteenth century and the first decades of this, have suffered a similar fate. Middle Hill House, the home of Colonel Leopold Paget, before he moved to Park Homer, stood among the trees to the north of Cannon Hill Road, and Olivers House, home of Major Eric Hanbury-Tracy, whose son, Claude, eventually inherited the Uddens Estate from his aunt, Mrs Oldfield, was nearly opposite the school in Middlehill Road. Olivers House was converted to a Home for Elderly People and renamed Stroud Lodge towards the end of its life. The names of two adjoining streets on the nearby housing estate remember both names of the old house.

Market gardens used to flourish on the slopes of Cannon Hill, down towards Canford Bottom, when it formed part of the Uddens Estate. Claude Hanbury-Tracy-Domville made a present of Church Moor Copse to the local council, to be preserved as an open-air amenity for the public, and is the home now of the local Scout Troop; and sold the remainder as building land. The area is now completely covered with houses, together with two more examples of what now seems to be Colehill's principal industry, Education. Nearly 80 teachers and more than 1300 children now attend the six schools in the village. No fewer than three of these are congregated in the Middlehill area, on the old Uddens Estate, within a couple of hundred yards of each other. Fashions in describing schools seem to be constantly changing: all three schools are what used to be known as "Elementary" Schools; we were taught later to call them "Primary" Schools; and the current fashion is "First" Schools. Middlehill School, the original village school, is now called Colehill, and the two new ones, built in the early 'seventies, are Hayeswood and St. Catherine's. Hayeswood dates from 1972 when David Lyne Coles was its first Head. Mrs June Watson succeeded him in 1989. St Catherine's, a Roman Catholic school, started life in 1973. Its early headmistresses were nuns, Sister Vincent and Sister Kathleen Murphy. Its status changed later from a "First" to a "Primary" school – to add to the confusion – and Mrs H. Bonser has been in charge since 1990.

Cannon Hill has retained its covering of pine trees, in the

custody of the Forestry Commission, which purchased much of the plantation and leased the remainder from Elizabeth Oldfield, who had inherited the Uddens Estate. The leased portion constitutes the last remnant, still owned by the Tracy family, of what had once been a great Estate, including the whole of the eastern part of Colehill and much of the parish of Hampreston, as well as land beyond the Stour in Canford Magna.

The Ordnance Survey uses the spelling "*Canon* Hill" in its earlier maps; and no record appears of any skirmishes in the Civil War on Cannon Hill. Yet the older spelling of the name, now in general use again, is suggestive, especially bearing in mind the folk-legend of the Soldier's Ring, said to be the burial ground of some of Cromwell's men, or those of Fairfax, on Jinny Down, and the harder (in both senses of the word) evidence of the discovery at Merrifield of a cannon ball dating from that period, now displayed at The Priest's House Museum in Wimborne. Gun-fire can still be heard at Cannon Hill – occasionally at week-ends – but nothing is fired in anger down at Pilford; the targets are not men but clay-pigeons. But, for much of the time, Cannon Hill remains an oasis of peace, the only traffic along what has been named "The Castleman Trailway" consisting of pedestrians, cyclists and horse-riders. It is pleasant that Charles Castleman should be remembered in this way, but the actual track-bed of the railway which he promoted – opened in 1847, when it became the main line between London and Dorchester, and closed in 1967 – lies half a mile away, in the bottom of the valley, to the south.

The bridle track along the spine of Cannon Hill formed part of the original route from Hampreston and Little Canford up to Colehill, but with the greater preponderance of wheeled traffic demanding a more modest gradient up the hill, a new road – our modern Canford Bottom and Middlehill Road – superceded the old one. This remains the domain of "joggers" and walkers, the latter often accompanied by dogs. The dogs generally seem to be enjoying the exercise more than their owners, and one gets the impression that it is the human beings who are being "taken walkies" by their dogs, rather than the other way about. Horse riders seem to keep to a sedate trot, with an occasional brisk canter to remind one of the old times when there was a race-course here, in the days of Nathaniel Gundry.

This account, with the date-line "Wimborne in Dorsetshire June 26", appeared in an issue of the Salisbury Journal in July 1756:

"On Thursday last was run for on a New Course at Cannon's Hill, near this Town, a Gentleman's Gift, for which Four Horses started, and was won by Mr King's Sorrel Gelding called Careless with some Difficulty. And Yesterday Five Horses started on the same Course for a Subscription Plate, which was won with Ease by Mr Steward's Mare Charming Nancy, and in the Evening there was a splendid Ball at the New Inn in Wimborne at which there was a great deal of Polite Company. . . ."

Among the archives of the Uddens Estate is a sort of occasional diary – a "Common Place Book: Records and Observations 1877". The handwriting varies in this manuscript account, and it is not always clear who is the actual writer. However, General Sir Edward Harris Greathed is clearly the author of an entry on 10 October 1878, in which he reminisces about his days as a colonel during the Indian Mutiny: "This is the anniversary of our fight at Agra in 1857 . . ." The following March, he records that he "has enclosed 42 acres on Cannon Hill Common". The estate built a new gravel highway, Pilford Lane, in 1879, and in the same year, the diary laments the death of Freeman from injuries received in a fall of earth in a gravel pit – "one of my best woodsmen". 23,000 trees – firs and hardwood – were planted in 1880. The Glyns were related to the Greatheds, and mention is made, in 1917, of the Sir Richard Glyn of the time: "Now 86, one of the few survivors of Balaclava", in which he served with the Royal Dragoons in the Heavy Brigade.

Elizabeth Oldfield, daughter of the renowned Sir Edward Greathed, inherited the large Uddens Estate, and was one of the last remnants of the rather feudal society which survived into the middle years of this century. She was one of the earliest motorists in the district, and most of the many anecdotes about her, few, alas, to her credit, are connected with her exploits at the wheel. Her laundrywomen were Mrs Habgood and Mrs

Mackrell, at Pilford, and they would be summoned to fetch and carry the washing by imperious blasts on the car's horn, as Mrs Oldfield waited in Lonnen Road.

At the foot of Cannon Hill ran the old railway, with level crossings both at Canford Bottom and Hayes Lane. Sansom was the crossing-keeper at the former, and Mrs Scrivens was in charge at Hayes. The standard practice was for the gates to be shut against road traffic. When a motorist wished to pass, he had to pull up and summon the gate-keeper by means of a push-button bell. Mrs Scrivens would eventually appear – sometimes, as the author can testify, not best pleased at having her domestic arrangements interrupted – to open the gates and then shut them again. Her predecessors at the Hayes Lane crossing were Mr and Mrs Mills, and George Oliver held office there, at the time of the 1891 census. His address is given as "Railway Lodge No. 22". One of his neighbours was the pedler hawker, Isaac Chewter, remembered by some of the very elderly as one of the village characters.

5
Top of The Hill

The village centre, in so far as it can be said to have a "centre" at all, lies at the top of the hill. This is still fairly rural in appearance, the modern housing estates having been mainly built on the slopes around it. This, at the top of the hill, was where the churches were built, the Anglican Church of St Michael and All Angels, erected in 1893, with its much more modern church school, the "Middle" school of St Michael's, next door; and the "new" Methodist Church, dating from 1913, in Lonnen Road, which took the place of the old mud-

Village outing to Cheddar probably early 1920s, to judge by the women's hats and the vintage char-a-banc.

Band of Hope char-a-banc outing 1927. Those sitting include, from the left, Harry and Mrs Richmond, Edie Wareham, Mrs Poore, Win Poore, Jessie Hall, Mrs Frampton, Vera Frampton and Sarah Rabbitts. Standing, from the left, are Mrs Green, Mrs Moody, Miss Short, Mrs Hall, Walt and Mrs Richmond, Maude Allen, Mr and Mrs Newman, Mrs Holder, Joyce Holder, Win Hall, Les Hall, Albert and Ray Holder, and Dorcas and Sylvia Habgood.

built church further down the road. The Post Office stands here at the cross-roads, and what remains of the local garage, bereft nowadays of its petrol pumps, is close at hand.

The centre of the village, in a social sense, though, is more difficult to locate. The church halls, Anglican and Methodist, it is true, are used by some local organisations, but the newer Memorial Hall and its near contemporary, the Public Library, are located half a mile away, near the original Village school, at Middlehill. The three public houses, *The Horns*, *The Barley Mow* and the newer *Sir Winston Churchill*, are even further away. The cricket ground is right on the edge of the village, just

[85]

The Firs. The scene appears to be near "The Slop", near the Church, looking towards the Post Office.

The Firs. It is difficult to date these photographs, probably about the turn of the century.

Left: ARP Wardens c. 1940. Frank Price, left, and Captain Baraud. Paget Cottages are on the right.

Below: "Casualty" unknown; those standing include Garney Williams, Captain Baraud, Maurice Hall and Frank Price, photographed in Kyrchil Lane.

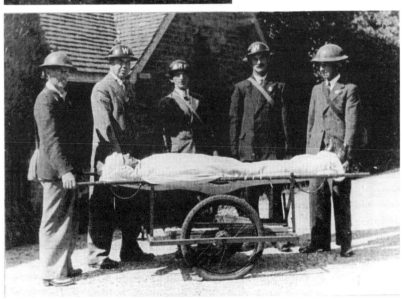

above Rowlands, and the football club shares a venue out at Gaunts Common, outside the village altogether.

However, by turning back the pages of history, it is clear that the centre of the village used to present a much livelier scene. David Cobb, who served on the Parish Council, and who was descended from the nineteenth century brickmaker, was a chiropodist who also doubled as the village barber – literally serving the community from head to foot – in a wooden building in the garden of his home in Wimborne Road, until the 1970s. His wife, Esme, ran a small drapery and footwear business from the same premises. Cobb's father, also David, had also been in business, as a boot and shoe retailer, and his custom had come from door-to-door sales, before he opened his shop. One hopes that the footwear was not so ill-fitting that his customers later in life became patients of his son! Reg Shiner, in his younger days a baker employed by Frank Barrett, later opened his shoe repair workshop behind his house in Holmsley Villas, with the other village cobbler, Frank Wareham, in business at Merrifield. Merrifield was also the location of the village wheelwright, another Wareham, and of the first village bakery, run by "Billy Tweet", William Barrett, Frank's father.

1st Colehill Girl Guides Company.

Left: Reg Shiner c. 1935

Below: Reg Shiner's Workshop, still standing in 1993, with enamel sign for shoe polish still preserved.

The village blacksmith, Joseph Edward Guy, having succeeded his father, Joseph Hardy Guy, who took over Colehill Farm soon after the Great War, carried on working at the little smithy in Colehill Lane for the rest of his life. The business closed when he died, during the 1939-45 war, after 40 years of ownership by the family. Both father and son were keen sportsmen, playing for the village cricket and football teams, both clubs then owning allegiance to the Church and both called Colehill St Michael's. The cricket club played on a field behind the smithy, owned by the elder Guy, in its early days, but moved, after the Great War, to "Mr Solly's field", its present home, although George Solly's descendants have long since gone from the area. The next generation of the Guy family kept up the connection with the cricket club, in the person of Archie, but he did not follow his father's trade. The local Boy Scout troop and the cubs used the old blacksmiths premises as a meeting place for some years before moving to their new headquarters at Churchmoor Copse.

The Guy family – "old" Joe, his wife Elizabeth and "young" Joe – owned and presided over the Coffee Tavern, a short

The Coffee Tavern, centre, and the old blacksmith's shop, on the left, Colehill Lane, c. 1991.

distance further down the hill from the forge. The corrugated iron building still survives, with its ghosts of lively days in the past, when it performed many functions, being the village hall of its time, and was, for very many years, until 1944, the meeting place of the Parish Council. The Men's Institute met there for recreation, the School used it for cookery lessons, "young" Joe and Charlie Matcham started their bicycle selling and repairing business there, and it was the changing room for the Football Club, with the elderly Elizabeth Guy providing hot baths for the players, after their game at Patey's, the field on the other side of the road. The Coffee Tavern was originally sited a few hundred yards away, in Lonnen Road, where it was located at the time of the 1885 Ordnance Survey. The building was physically removed to its present situation around the time the Guys came to live in the village.

The infamous and perhaps rather over-romanticised smuggling trade is recalled in the name of the road running down the hill from the Church, past the Old Vicarage, Smugglers Lane; it was indeed one of the well-used smuggling routes, as testified by a villager in the last century. However, Kipling's "Brandy for the Parson, Baccy for the Clerk" would hardly have rung true in later years, as Cyril Kindersley, the first Vicar of Colehill, seems to have been of a rather abstemious disposition, judging by his support for the temperance movement. An alternative name for Smugglers Lane, once in common usage, Brick Hill, recalls the old Coombes brick-works here, before the Great War, some of whose products were used in the building of the church.

Behind the church, where the playing fields of St Michael's School now extend almost as far as Wimborne Road, was an area of woodland and open heath, where donkies used to graze, known as Jenny Down. Colehill Pond, once much loved by the young people of the village as a skating rink in season, disappeared when yet another new school, Beaucroft School, was built in 1974. The clump of trees known as Soldiers Ring, from a folk legend based perhaps on historical fact, and the two Bronze Age round barrows have been preserved.

Evidence of a rather more modern piece of Colehill's history can be seen by the observant beside the road between the

War Memorial and the Post Office, the foundations of the old Iron Church, "Trotman's Tin Tabernacle", which served as a place of worship in the ten years preceding the building of St Michael's. Efforts to trace the subsequent physical history of the Iron Church have been unsuccessful. It has been suggested that it was removed to the New Forest, but the most likely fate seems to have been that it was broken up and portions sold to (or otherwise appropriated by) local pig farmers.

St. Michael's Church. This must be the earliest photograph of the church. It was completed and dedicated in December 1893 and consecrated in June 1895. The Consecration ceremony could not be carried out until all debts on the building had been cleared. This enables us to date the photograph with some precision as the notice is still appealing for funds. The wording is not easy to decipher but appears to read: "Subscriptions to the Building Fund are earnestly requested. £290 needed to clear the debt. Subscriptions received by Mrs Paget, Park Homer, & Gen Robert Truell".

St. Michael's Church c. 1905.

St. Michael's Church c. 1903, before the erection of the Church Hall.

[93]

The history of St Michael and All Angels Church, which has now celebrated its centenary, is fairly well documented elsewhere. It was inspired by Colonel Leopold Paget, who moved from Middle Hill House to live at Park Homer with his wife, Georgiana, and his large family, two at least of whom were subsequently to achieve fame as soldiers. Harold, the eldest son, raised "Paget's Horse" as a colonel during the Boer War, and Wellesley, who rose to the rank of Brigadier-General, served both in South Africa and during the Great War. The old colonel, having been invalided out of the Army following injuries sustained in the Indian Mutiny, during which he made the acquaintance of Colonel Greathed, retired to Dorset and more peaceful pursuits, and devoted his energies to the funding and building of the Colehill Church. He died, alas, in 1892, before building was begun. The church, designed by W.D. Caroe, is of sufficient interest to attract an entry – "Nice little essay in Arts and Crafts style . . . Brick, half-timber and plaster. Interior like a timbered barn" – in John Betjeman's Guide to English Parish Churches, one of fewer than 70 selected from

St. Michael's Church c. 1990, with the hall on the left.

George Thorne and his wife, outside the porch of St Michael and All Angels c. 1900. Thorne, who died in 1911, was for many years the caretaker and sexton of St Michael's, and, earlier, of the Iron Church. Three of his grandchildren, George, Mabel and Nellie, appear in the photographs of the scholars of Middle Hill School.

Dorset. Externally, there has been little change to the building, while inside, the march of progress has been marked over the years by improved lighting, from the original oil lamps, through the acetylene and gas eras to electricity. Plaques honouring locally well-known benefactors, the Pagets, the Truells, Mrs Lees and so on, adorn the walls, and the cross marking the battlefield grave of Arthur Lonsdale at Neuve Chapelle now rests in the church. Lonsdale's mother, a member of the Glyn family, lived at The Further House, now called Joldwynds, and was prominent in village affairs.

Kindersley, the first Vicar of St Michael's, initiated much of the social and sporting activity in the village, being instrumental in the formation of both the Cricket and Football Clubs. He was a good cricketer and the Club's first Captain. He was a good patriot too, as witnessed by his spending an entire summer working on a farm at Winterborne Kingston during the food crisis in the Great War, and subsequently giving up the Living permanently to serve at the Front with the Church Army. Arthur Stote, his successor at Colehill, spent much time researching local history, and some of the fruits of his labours, recorded in the Parish Magazine, have benefitted later historians. Stote later changed his name to incorporate that of his wife's family and became Stote-Blandy. These two, Kindersley and Stote-Blandy, served the church for its first 53 years. They were followed in succession by John Price, W.L. Dobb, Charles

Mrs Kindersley, wife of the first Vicar of Colehill.

Colehill Mothers's Union c. 1912. Vera Richmond and Beryl Shiner are 3rd and 6th from the left in the front row; second row, l. to r.: ?, ?, Mrs Christopher, ?, Mrs Ethel Shiner, with Rex Shiner on her lap, Mrs Kindersley (holding dog), Mrs Moore – later to become Mrs Cobb, Mrs Hall, ?, ?; Mrs Augustus Richmond and Mrs Emily Habgood are 2nd and 3rd from the left in the third row; Mrs Dacombe, Mrs Coombes and Mrs Green are 2nd, 4th and 5th from the left in the back row.

Raynor-Smith, the ex-Royal Navy officer, who has continued to serve the church elsewhere in his retirement, Michael Jeffrey, especially remembered for his ministry to the deaf, who died tragically in office, and the present incumbent, John Goodall.

The clergy have been supported down the years by a host of laymen (and women). One cannot name them all, but prominent among them were the gentry in the early years, Mrs Georgiana Paget, the Colonel's widow, and Mrs Bernarda Lees. Frank Barrett, postmaster, baker, hire car proprietor (and driver), Chairman of the Parish Council, treasurer of both the Cricket and Football Clubs (and trainer of the latter), comedian and leading light in almost every club and society in the village – it seems that the only organisations to which he did not belong were the Women's Institute and the Mothers' Union! – was a chorister and Parochial Church Councillor. One of his comic stories, a trifle irreverent, certainly in those days for an audience consisting largely of churchgoers, has come down through the years. The reference is to the road running beside the cricket ground – "There's that line in the old hymn: 'There is a green hill far away'. Far away? Why, I can throw a cricket ball further than Greenhill".

The Digby sisters, Edith and Mabel; Herbert Senior; Sir Richard Glyn, fifth Baronet; Sister D.R. Dare, the local District Nurse; Frank Middleton, honoured for gallantry during the 1939-45 war; Stanley Weedon; Charles Osborne, the retired Commodore, who had the distinction of escorting into Liverpool the first U-Boat to be captured in the Great War; Charlie Sawtell; Garney Williams; Percy Shearing; "Jimmy" Hewett, distinguished also in the Girl Guide movement locally; Roly Raymond; Jack Cassell; George Gray, still active in church affairs – these and many others have given their time and talents to St Michael's. One of them, Miss Kathleen Fell, a remarkable elderly woman, will be remembered driving her ancient Austin A 30 around the village. She was the victim one night of an attempted burglary: she accosted the intruder, who immediately beat a hasty retreat empty-handed!

There has been a choral tradition throughout the lifetime of the church; among the choristers are the long-serving Alec Moore and Barbara Roberts who alone remain from the time of Stote, having survived a multitude of organists. The best remembered of these was Bernard Russell who raised the standard of the music to a splendid level. Of the lay readers, Rupert Keable and Ronald Fletcher, both fine preachers, are especially remembered with much affection.

One of the greatest benefits – some may argue *the* greatest benefit – which the church has brought to the village was to beget the new school next-door. This was the first of the new schools to be built on Colehill, opened in 1971 with the bearded Martin Neeves as Headmaster. Malcolm Chisholm succeeded Neeves in 1985. Andrew Jones, the deputy Head, has

Part of the St. Michael's School Orchestra c. 1987. Andrew Jones is in the front row, centre right.

been in charge of the School's music from its earliest days and has fashioned a highly talented orchestra from the successive relays of students in his care. And so the rich musical tradition of the village, going back for a hundred years, continues to flourish.

The middle of the village is occupied by a wooded triangle, owned by the National Trust, successors in title to the Bankes Estate. The church stands at one of the corners, the Post Office at another; and prominent at the third is the War Memorial. The observant will notice, apart from the names of the men, that the word "Colehill" is recessed. Fear of a German invasion in 1940 caused the authorities to order all place names, on road-signs and elsewhere, to be expunged; the village name on the Memorial thus had to be chiselled away, and was not restored until after the war. At one time, Emma Habgood had run one of Colehill's many laundries from premises nearly opposite the site of the old Iron Church. Many years later, Lewis started a sweet shop at this address. He later installed petrol pumps and so began what became the Colehill Service Station. The business, still quite a small one, was sold to the

Colehill Mini Supermarket c. 1974.

Colehill Post Office c. 1905. Harry Newman stands at the door of the shop, with Mrs Barrett (probably) on the left.

Smugglers Lane, looking towards the church, c. 1905. The Post Office is on the extreme right.

Drinkwaters in the 'fifties, but was extensively enlarged when Ron Jones took it over, and he added an off-license in an adjoining building. This later became the short-lived "Colehill Mini-market", opened by Bob and Yvonne Sims in 1974.

Frank Barrett was the first to start a business on this site, in the closing years of the last century, and moved his bakery a few yards along the road to the cross-roads, where he opened the village Post Office, in 1896. He remained the Postmaster, and ran the general stores there until the early years of the second war. The business stayed in the family when Barrett died, because his daughter, Amy, wife of the farmer Claude Roberts, succeeded him. Many will recall the old small, ill-lit shop of those days, brought so vividly to life in Nell Tilley's playlet, referred to elsewhere in this book. When John and Mary Dacombe took over the shop and Post Office, they modernised and extended the premises.

The house opposite the Post Office, now renamed, was once called The Priory, but whether this had any significance or was merely the whim of the owner is not known. A short distance down the hill, in Lonnen Road, stands the "new"

The Post Office and Smugglers Lane, looking towards the church. "F. Barrett maker of Hovis" is clearly visible above the shop window, but it is less easy to decipher the other advertisements: "Brooke Bond Tea", "Brown & Polson Paisley Flour" and "Peak Frean's Teddy Bear biscuits". It is possible to date the picture accurately as September 1921 from the wording of the two notices – "Church Parade – Broadstone Sub-branch United Ex-Servicemen. Sunday, Sept 26th. Poole Town Band." and "Football Match. 25th Sept Colehill St Michael v. Wimborne Town."

Methodist Church, sustained down the years by, among others, the Moody and Habgood families, John and Molly Slow, Pat and Marjorie Cailes, Edna Shave and its first resident minister, the deaconess Pamela Le Poidevin – "Sister Pam" to many.

Middlehill Road, running between the Post Office and Middlehill School, was the boundary between the Glyn Estate, remembered in the local name Glynville, and the Park Homer Estate. A substantial wood of pines covered the ground to the north, but much of the woodland was cleared in the late 1920s to make room for the first council houses to be built on Colehill. Nearby, in Marianne Road, Mary Short did brisk business as one of the many local laundresses. Her customers

"The Priory" c. 1905. The house – renamed – still stands, opposite the Post Office, on the extreme left.

Colehill Methodist Chapel 1913. Fund-raising garden party for the new building.

Colehill Methodist Chapel. Opening ceremony 1913.

Mary Short, outside her laundry in Marianne Road 1905.

Left: Pat O'Hara c. 1955.

Below: The Beeches 1924. This was built by Herbert Habgood, and became his home. It stands completely isolated in the narrow, gravelled Middlehill Road, looking towards the school.

were mainly the local gentry, and much of the laundry would consist of maid-servants' uniforms, which would need to be starched and ironed, as well as washed, and the caps and cuffs crimped with a pair of gophers. After the war, the first purpose-built Police House was erected in Middlehill Road, with PC O'Hara – baptised Alfred but "Pat" to his fellow cricketers and other friends in the village – as its first resident.

PCs Webber, Doug Legg and Roy Hurd in turn succeeded O'Hara at the house. Eventually it passed into private ownership, but its former function is remembered in the felicitous naming of the house as "Peelers". Cobb's Orchard stood back from the road, behind the Police House. Weston Road remembers the name of a former resident, Jack, who used to thunder away in the bass line of the Church choir 30 years ago.

Across the road, an ancient stone, standing until a few years ago, marked the site of Elliotts Grave. No reliable evidence remains as to who Elliott might have been: local folklore has it variously that he was either a criminal, hanged here, or a suicide. His Grave was certainly marked on maps and referred to in legal documents dating back more than two centuries to identify a specific geographical point in what, at that time, was featureless barren heath country; an alternative identification was used, "The Three Lords Lands", indicating that this was where the estates of the three great local landowners, Bankes, Hanham and Lord Arundell, met. Behind what is now the small parade of shops, lay Park Homer House, in grounds so extensive at one time that the Estate was second only to that of Beaucroft in area. This was the home of the illustrious Paget family for 60 years, up until the end of the Great War. They were followed by the tall, distinguished-looking Mrs Farrer, always dressed in black, who, in the fashion of the time, expected the curtsies of the village girls and women and the doffing of caps by the boys and men; she had the reputation of being "a terror" to her servants, none of whom stayed more than a few days.

Park Homer House was empty by 1950 and was converted into flats for the homeless before being demolished in the mid-fifties. The grounds had been sold off gradually over the preceding years in small building plots. Park Homer Road, Park Homer Drive and Paget Close remember the old house and the Colonel's family who once lived there. The old cottage, occupied by Paget's gardener, Hebditch, still remains and the colourful blooms which adorn the way down the hill to Leigh Lane each succeeding summer survive from the famous Rhododendron Drive, now part footpath and part roadway. This part of Colehill has become a sort of "Harley Street" in miniature, the location chosen by a succession of Wimborne medical practitioners for their homes – but not their surgeries: they are in the town.

Eccentric characters vividly recalled from the past abound in the memories of the villagers: Frances Bliss, the nocturnal gardener and writer of poetry; Bailey, the chimney sweep from Sandy Lane; the enthusiastic pedestrian from Highland Road, constantly walking to and fro, known simply as "Mr Walker Man"; Addie Street, who used to collect and deliver the laundry of the "Big" Houses for various washerwomen; Fred Angel, the long-serving gardener at The Croft; and the tall, rather taciturn resident at Joldwynds of some 30 years ago. He, apparently, expected letters addressed simply to "Colonel Gray, Colehill" to reach him; alas, the Post Office chose instead to deliver much of his mail to another Colonel Gray, perhaps better-known, and also living in the village – George of that ilk. And eccentric characters did not go out of fashion in mid-century: they still thrive. People achieve a certain anonymity, if not invisibility, when riding in motor cars, so it is the pedestrians that one recalls as "characters". I would refrain from mentioning names, even if I knew them, for fear of causing offence – not everyone likes to be thought of as a "character". And, to me, they remain "Foggy" and "Pork-pie" and the rest!

Colehill Cricket Club 1911. Standing, l. to r. F. Ives snr (Umpire), Reg Welch, Walt Richmond, E. Osman, Joe Guy snr, F. Ives jnr, Harry Richmond, Henry Habgood; sitting, l. to r. R. Hall, Joe Guy jnr, J. Hall, "Bossy" Cole.

6

Writers of The Hill

It seems that no William Shakespeare or Charles Dickens has emerged from the pinewoods of Colehill – although, indeed, the first Churchwarden of Colehill, Mrs Georgiana Paget, was descended from Anne Agar, née Milton, the youngest sister of the poet John Milton. However, the village has been home to a not inconsiderable number of writers over the years.

The first of whom we have any knowledge is William Kingston, born in 1814 in Harley Street, London, who might be said to have been the originator of the Anglican Church on Colehill. He is listed in the 1851 Census as a "writer of general literature" living at Middlehill, and he it was who originated the idea of "reading the afternoon service" to the villagers, a custom later revived by Colonel Leopold Paget, of Park Homer House, whose energy and enthusiasm (and money) were eventually to inspire the building, first, of the Iron Church, and then its successor, St Michael's.

Charles Hay, who lived at Deans Grove and later at Rowney House, was the brother-in-law of the first Vicar of Colehill, Cyril Kindersley. Hay was a keen sportsman and very active in the affairs of the village. He was a field sports enthusiast, excelling with the gun, but he suffered a severe back injury while hunting. He was a particularly good friend, from the time of their formation, to the village cricket and football clubs, both of which were originally named Colehill St Michael's. He was the author of a book entitled *Merle of the Wessex Hills* which, it is believed, was published privately. This work, rubbing shoulders with those of such literary giants as William Barnes and Thomas Hardy, is listed in the bibliography of Dorset which used to be published in the Dorset Year Books in the late 'twenties. The book, a novelette, has been described by a surviving relative as "good on language and grammar" but – perhaps a little unkindly – "weak on plot".

Two other Colehill writers contributed to the Year Book itself around that time. Nell Tilley, who lived in a bungalow at Green Bottom, was a bird-lover and a keen observer of wild-life in general, and contributed a series of articles on those subjects to the Year Book. One article dealt at some length with one particular bird, a Great Spotted Woodpecker, which fed regularly in her garden, and also frequented the Vicarage garden, where its activities could be heard during services by the congregation at St Michael's Church. This prompted a letter to The Times by the Vicar, Arthur Stote, which seems to have started a considerable correspondence in that paper, to which Mrs Maud Hay, wife of Charles, also contributed. Miss Tilley, who ran a newsagency in East Street, Wimborne, was also the author of some Dorset dialect verse – "Changes" – which appeared in one issue of the Dorset Year Book. Her literary talents included the writing of at least one short, amusing play, "Our Village Shop". The characters are, of course, all fictional, but represent a fair cross-section of village society in 1930. It needs little imagination for the scene to be set in Colehill Post Office and to recognise some of the local characters from more than 60 years ago, and, no doubt, some of the more elderly villagers could readily supply the name of an actual person for each member of the cast. "Mrs Croker", the shopkeeper in the play, having sold some penny and halfpenny stamps to "Fussy Old Lady", enquires if there is "Anything more?", to which the answer is "A pennyworth of soda and a pennyworth of salt, please, and send it up by your boy today certain". This short extract indicates the humour of the piece, and also reflects some of the attitudes of the times. An acting fee of half-a-crown was charged for performing the play, with the proceeds going to the Wimborne Cottage Hospital.

Frances Bliss was the author of several poems included in the Year Books during that time. She was a versatile writer, her work ranging from the sombre, almost mystical, to the amusing "The Winterbourne Where Albert Stayed". She was, however, probably at her best in her descriptive writing, "Hills of Dor-set", for example, and the rather emotive verses which describe the felling of the pine trees on Colehill, from which I quoted an extract in my history of the village, *Village on the Hill*. This poem was printed under the title of "Colehill, 1929", but I have a copy of the relevant Year Book owned by Miss Bliss in which she has attached a written note to the pages on which her poem appears: "Title RESURGAM *not* Colehill 1929". The alteration was presumably an afterthought, as it could scarcely have been such an inspired printer's error. Miss Bliss had an elder spinster sister, Louise Maria, who was the Principal of the Melverley Girls' School. Frances came to live in Leigh Lane, overlooking Leigh Vineries and witnessed the demolition of the acres of glass-houses about 1960, and their replacement by a housing estate. Thus it was that I became her next-door neighbour – just one field away – and so became acquainted with her. She lived to a great age, something of a recluse and an eccentric towards the end, surrounded by a large family of stray cats which she had befriended. It was her invariable custom to sleep out of doors, on her verandah, in all weathers, no matter how cold or inclement. When sleep eluded her, she is said to have got up and tended her garden, by the light of a hurricane lamp.

John Haime, who lived near Middlehill School (now called Colehill County First), was the author of a privately published book, *The Haimes of Dorset*, a lively account of his family history, in which he records with much relish the various stages of his researches. Among his other talents was the production of an exquisite blackcurrant wine, almost a liqueur, which I was privileged to sample when I made his acquaintance.

Mildred Gillett was never a resident of Colehill, but must be included in this list as she was a prominent figure in the village, being the Headmistress of Middlehill School during those years of expansion in the 'sixties when the population, largely of young families, grew so rapidly, and Middlehill remained the only school in the village, its roll increasing from 150, in 1955, to nearly 450, when she retired in 1969. In her retirement, Miss Gillett has written *Talbot Village*, an account of the Estate in Bournemouth established by Georgina Talbot.

Rev Robert Garrard, Vicar, for several years, of St John's, Wimborne, British and Foreign Bible Society Secretary for the

Use and Study of the Bible, actively associated with the Shaftesbury Society, and resident of Colehill, who frequently "stood in" at St Michael's during temporary absences of the Vicar, Charles Raynor-Smith, is the author of *Why read the Bible*. Ronald Fitzmaurice, the manager of a local bank, was another of the village authors. He was a man of many and varied interests, among which was the writing of *British Banks and Banking – a Pictorial History*, a lucid and most interesting account, copiously illustrated, going back to the earliest times, long before the days of "The Big Five" and then "The Big Four". Stanley Lodge, active on the Parochial Church Council of St Michael's for many years, was a playwright whose entertaining *Generation Trap* was first performed by the Wimborne Drama Club a few years ago.

Mention must also be made of two privately produced booklets commemorating anniversaries of the two local Methodist Churches, Ralph Habgood – who, for much of his lifetime, has been, following in the footsteps of his father, Henry, prominent in the affairs of the Colehill Cricket Club, both as player and secretary – recording the centenary of the Broomhill Wesleyan Methodist Church, and Mrs Marjorie Cailes celebrating the 75th anniversary of the "new" Primitive Methodist Church on Colehill.

Edna Shave was the author of several poems, ranging in mood from the amusing "Darzet Wedden'" to the melancholy and perhaps introspective "The Passing". Miss Shave, a teacher of drama and literature, came to live on Colehill in 1964, and became prominent in the worship of both the Methodist and Anglican Churches. In her later years, this remarkable woman became a graduate of the Open University, with a BA degree, and I was privileged to join her in founding a local poetry-reading circle. This, happily, has continued to thrive down the years, fostered by Howard and Barbara Simpson, and the group had the felicitous idea, when Miss Shave died in 1992, of producing a slim volume of her verse, to perpetuate her memory. She is remembered also in a window at the front of the Methodist Church, depicting a dove, emblem of peace, and the cross, but not – which seems a pity – recording her name. Alan Bennett, namesake of a rather better-known writer

The Edna Shave Memorial Window in the Methodist Chapel 1994. Miss Shave lived directly across the road from the chapel at Willow Cottage, part of which can be seen through the window, on the left.

(and actor), is one of the latest of our village authors, having recently contributed to the extensive literature on Wimborne. He also wrote *Horsewoman*, a biography of Louie Dingwall, the Sandbanks race-horse trainer.

Another writer – with a prolific output – is Roger Guttridge, contributing regularly to the columns of the Bournemouth Evening Echo and the Southern Evening Echo of Southampton, as well as writing for the Dorset Magazine. After 20 years as a newspaper journalist at Yeovil and Bournemouth, he became a freelance writer and is the author of several books of local interest. *Dorset Smugglers* was his first book, to be followed by *Dorset Murders, Ten Dorset Mysteries, Hampshire Murders, Blackmore Vale Camera, The Landscapes of Dorset*, the *Evening Echo Book of Heritage in Dorset and the New Forest* and *The Villages of Dorset*. He is also the co-author of the official publication produced to mark the 50th anniversary of the "D-Day" landings in Normandy. Guttridge was also responsible for unearthing and publishing a literary relic more than 100 years old

– and this must surely rank as not the least of his achievements. *Six Men on the Stour*, written by one of the "six", Ernest Brett, familiarly known as "Skipper" Brett, who came to live on Colehill, was a record of a journey from Wimborne to Mudeford, inspired, one might guess, by Jerome's *Three Men in a Boat*. The fascinating story of how the account of this Victorian voyage remained in manuscript form and did not see the light of day until 1983 is told by Guttridge in an introduction to the book, which he published two years later.

Dr Alexander Wierzbicki has written a biography of the illustrious Czar of Russia, Peter the Great, founder of the city of St Petersburg, and conqueror of much of eastern Europe. This historical work is in Russian and therefore unlikely to find many local readers in its present form, although a translation into English is pending. Wierzbicki graduated as a Doctor of Philosophy from a university in his native Poland. His fascinating account of his subsequent wartime adventures would have made compelling reading, if he had chosen to record it: he eventually joined the Polish Army and served with their Corps alongside the British Eighth Army in the Western Desert and Italy, before settling in England after the war, and latterly making his home on Colehill.

Another Colehill resident, however, has left a record of his wartime career, when he served with distinction with Coastal Command of the RAF, the most unsung branch of the service. Des Curtis, DFC, is the author of *A Most Secret Squadron*, a history, hitherto unrecorded, of 618 Squadron. Curtis, a navigator, and his pilot, previously flying in Bristol Beaufighters, were founder members of the new squadron, formed shortly after 617 – the "Dambusters". 618, equipped with de Havilland Mosquitoes, had a similar mission, a low level attack on the German battleship *Tirpitz*, using the Barnes Wallis "bouncing bomb". A Special Detachment of the squadron was later deployed against the U-boats operating from St Nazaire and other French and Norwegian ports. It was on one of these missions that both Curtis, a 19 year-old Flight Lieutenant at the time, and his pilot were awarded the DFC, when the U-boat U976 was sunk. There were 47 survivors from the submarine, including the captain, Oberleutnant

Raymond Tiesler, and a happy postscript to this story is that Curtis and Tiesler became friends after the war and remain so more than 50 years after their first encounter. A Freeman of the City of London and an accountant by profession, Curtis became prominent in the oil industry before retiring to Colehill to write the epic account of his war. The most recent recruit to Colehill's regiment of authors is Roly Hickes, now engaged in writing the history of the Colehill Cricket Club.

Epilogue

This account of Colehill over the last century (or two) is based almost entirely on what many of the villagers have remembered from their youth, and most of the illustrations also date back to their younger days. It seems almost incredible to realise how much has changed in a hundred years, or within living memory, say 80 years, which would take us back to the days of that terrible Great War which mercifully came to an end in 1918.

Colehill was not unique: although not a typical English village, nevertheless it might be regarded as a microcosm of rural England. A child in 1916 would have walked along gravel roads, with no sidewalks, where today nearly all the roads in the village are surfaced with tarmacadam, with paved footpaths; young Hanbury-Tracy went to Eton, but most of his contemporaries in the village, a lot of them ill-shod, splashing along through the mud and the puddles, went to Middlehill School. There were no school busses then, and the very few motor cars belonged to the well-to-do, such as the Digby, Hay and Solly families.

So the roads would have been quite peaceful, unlike today's, with constant traffic pounding along Middlehill Road and Wimborne Road – much of it exceeding the prescribed speed limit of 30 m.p.h.; the skies too would have been quieter and emptier, in spite of the activities of the Royal Flying Corps flying from their airfields on Salisbury Plain, with nothing taking-off or landing at the fields which were to become Hurn Airport. Even the gardens would have been quiet, compared with today's: villagers wielding their forks and spades, with none of the modern noisy, intrusive gadgetry. Water did not come out of a tap in the kitchen or bathroom – except for the few, who lived in the mansions and for others living at the top of the hill; it had to be drawn from a well behind the cottage, if you were lucky. If you were unlucky, you had to walk some distance and carry the water home in a pail, just as Jack and Jill did. Lighting and heating did not come at the touch of a switch: electricity had not reached the village; neither had gas, apart from the favoured area, connected with the mains, laid in the upper part of the village. You cooked on an old coke-fired range, you got warm from a coal fire, and you saw your way about on dark winter's nights by oil lamps and candles. The night skies over Colehill must have been very dark, for there was no street lighting. As for sewerage, mains drains did not reach even Wimborne for another 40 years or more.

There was no public transport in the village; on the other hand, you could travel to London – although only a few would have done so – by railway, after a half-hour walk to Wimborne Station. And, if you lived, say, in Wimborne Road, you had a choice of shops where you could buy your daily bread, fresh baked, and your groceries. They would be delivered to your own door, if you wished.

Society was rigidly class-conscious: you would not have met Mrs Truell buying her butter and cheese in Burling's grocery shop; and you would have been extremely surprised to meet Mrs Paget in the Post Office. You would, however, have probably seen some of the local gentry on a Sunday at St Michael's, attending Matins.

It is, however, the landscape that has changed most. A great number of open fields have been built over; much of the woodland, once such a characteristic of Colehill, has given place to houses and bungalows; and yet more building has replaced a great deal of the heathland, as at Pilford, and covers the sites of what were once the many market gardens and nurseries. Several of the large houses have been pulled down and their sites and grounds filled in with more modest property. The grand carriage entrance to Park Homer House has become the car park for Gwynne's newsagency.

Paradoxically, one is surprised at how much the village is unchanged. Much of the rural scene remains intact, not least in the centre of the village. In a comfortable walk of half an hour, up and across the hill from my home in Leigh Lane, I can find myself, if not in deep country, at least in pastoral surroundings, as far as the eye can see.

Researching and writing a local history, or a reminiscent book such as this, is rather like composing a picture from a jig-saw puzzle, with two million pieces. You start off with a general idea of what the picture will eventually look like; but you are never quite sure where to look for the next piece. Some you search for diligently, and, after much time and trouble, you find; others are conveniently handed to you by willing collaborators. But some elusive pieces you will never find, and so the picture is never *quite* finished.

However, having turned over every stone, you think you have finished the job to the best of your ability, and you get the book printed and presented to the public. Just at this point, some impish gremlin finds you one more piece of the jig-saw: I know because it has happened to me on a previous occasion! And now, with the bulk of this work having just gone to press, it has happened again! But, as a sort of postscript to the second chapter, I am able to add a little more to the stories of both Beaucroft and Bells. I am indebted to descendants of Mrs Bernarda Lees; and of George Solly, who have recalled childhood memories of the village.

Mrs Iris Rocksborough-Smith, born at Beaucroft in 1906, and blessed with a remarkable memory, is the grand-daughter of Mrs Lees. Eight children were born of the marriage of Thomas and Bernarda Lees before the move to Dorset, following the death of Thomas. There were three sons, the first of whom, Elliott, was created a baronet, while the other two died in infancy. The five daughters were Gracia, Eveline, Flora, Catherine and Dorothea (known familiarly as Dolly). Eveline married Colonel Laurence Parke, and they had a family of five, three sons and two daughters, the younger of whom was Iris. The Parke family returned to Beaucroft to manage affairs during the last two years of Mrs Lees' life, after she had suffered a stroke. Life at Beaucroft seems to have been lived on a grand scale, in more senses than one. Before her illness, Mrs Lees staged a production of Tchaikovski's ballet *The Sleeping Beauty*, in the House, in which all her grand-children had a part; and Shakespeare's play *A Midsummer Night's Dream* was performed in the woods behind the House. Mrs Rocksborough-Smith's vivid childhood memories clearly go back to the days before the Great War. She recalls the rigid social distinctions of those days, when even the family doctor, calling to attend to some illness in the house, was expected to use the tradesmen's entrance. No doubt, Kaye (later Sir Kaye) le Fleming, the celebrated Wimborne medical practitioner and

The Lees family. Bernarda, with her five daughters, Dorothea (Dolly), in her arms, and, clockwise, from top right, Eveline, Flora, Catherine (Kitty) and Gracia, c. 1880.

[119]

George and Helen (Nellie) Solly, with their coachman and "Dandy", c. 1893.

historian, was permitted the use of the front door, when he later became the family's physician. Amusing anecdotes include the story of the marriage of the chilren's nanny to the butler at Beaucroft, when young Iris was a bridesmaid. Nanny had suddenly changed colour because Miss Brown had become Mrs Green. Then there was the time when Moore, the coachman, announced that the family would be unable to enjoy their usual coach outing. "Why not?", he was asked.

"Because the mare's had a fall".

"How did that happen, then?"

It eventually transpired, after a correct interpretation of the Dorset dialect, that the mare had actually produced a foal!

Mrs Lees was early in having an alternative to horse-drawn transport, owning one of the first motor cars in the village, a Hotchkiss.

Iris Parke used to indulge in the adventurous pastime of placing a penny on the railway line and retrieving the squashed coin after the passage of a train. This was a popular children's sport for those who lived near the railway, and the Northleigh Lane bridge would have been a convenient point of access, nicely hidden from official gaze round the curve from Wimborne Station. She still carries visible evidence of one such escapade, bearing an 80-year old scar on her knee from an injury sustained in a fall as she rushed down the hill to the line on the rough gravel track that Beaucroft Lane then was.

Miss Dendy is remembered as one of the village characters, driving around Colehill in her pony and trap, with her Jack Russell for company.

Edward Solly owned much land at Parkstone and most of Sandbanks, but it was his son, George, who became the first owner of Bells House. He became prominent in village affairs when he moved into the house, with his bride, Helen Peake. There were three sons, Eddie, who died young, Rex and Noel, who spent much of his life in Kenya and married Gillian Olivier, related to the celebrated actor, Laurence (who, it seems, was the only member of that family to have adopted the French pronunciation of his surname).

Rex, who rose to the rank of Lieut Colonel in the Royal Corps of Signals, had three sons, George, John and David, all of whom spent part of their childhood at Bells, before the house and the rest of the twelve-acre estate was sold in 1950. Both George and John have recalled childhood memories of staying at Bells with their grandmother during the 1939-45 war. They remember her entertaining the air-crew who flew the Halifax glider tugs based at Tarrant Rushton; officers of the King's Dragoon Guards, whose tanks were kept on the wooded triangle between the Church, the Post Office and the War Memorial, being billeted at Bells; the servants at the House, Hopkins, the gardener, Kitty Vine, the parlourmaid, and the chauffeur Ernest Way, whose wife was a maid. There was a peculiar inconsistency in that, while he was normally addressed as "Ernest", she was always known only by her maiden surname, Orton. They remembered the Truells and the Rugge-Prices; and, above all, Charles Hay, described as quite a character and rather "larger than life". They could not, of course, remember their grandfather, the first George Solly. Active in

George Solly 1924.

village affairs, a lawyer, but not in practice, he seems to have
been a gentleman of leisure. He was known as a good shot and
a fine athlete. He played cricket for the newly formed Colehill
St Michael's club in 1905, and was its first President. He was
one of those elected to serve on the newly formed Parish
Council in 1896. He became Chairman in 1902 and served in

that capacity until his resignation shortly before his death in 1930.

The ecclesiastical parish of Colehill is more than 93 years old; the church itself has already celebrated its centenary, as has the civil parish. The village has managed to maintain its separate identity down the years in spite of repeated attempts by covetous neighbours to annexe it. The annals of the Parish Council record the various efforts, successfully resisted, to take over the village or for it to merge with one of its adjoining parishes. Nor was Wimborne the only town with such ambitions: not many years ago, a prominent sign was erected beside the main road at Leigh Common, informing east-bound traffic that it had reached Ferndown! The sign was removed after a few weeks and resited a mile further along the road. The Village Fathers, Solly and the others, have done well to preserve the integrity of Colehill through the years and continue to do so, displaying that unyielding obstinacy, so characteristic of the West Country, to all such proposals. There used to be a saying in my native county: "Wiltshire won't be druv". No, neither will Dorset be "druv". Nor yet Colehill in Dorset.

Bournemouth West to Salisbury train, hauled by Class T7 locomotive, approaching Northleigh Lane Bridge. Part of the Wimborne Gas Works can be seen above the rear coach. Photographed by Brian Kohring 1952.

The End of the Line. Bridge no. 74 carries Northleigh Lane over the railway. This photograph was taken in 1964, four months after the withdrawal of all passenger services. One track was removed soon afterwards, and the remaining one carried traffic to the Army Petroleum Depot at West Moors for another three years, before the line closed completely. Reproduced here by kind permission of Len Tavender, who published it originally in his book Southampton Ringwood Dorchester Railway, *one of the series of* Ringwood Papers.

Index

Cox, George 17-8
Cox, Harry 18
Cox, Kate 17
Cox, Sidney 59
Crichel House 55
Cricket Club 7, 31, 35, 44, *45*,
  47-8, 56, 66, 85, 90, 95,
  97-8, 105, *108*, 109, 112,
  115, 122
Croft 107
Cromwell, Oliver 63, 81
Cullen, Herbert 25, 72, *74*
Cullen, Les *71*
Cummings, George 9-10, 14
Curtis, Des 114-5
Curtler, Kathy 25
Curtler, Martyn 25
Dacombe, Alfred 33, 65, 78
Dacombe, Alice 33, *42*
Dacombe, Edgar 63
Dacombe, Gertie *42*
Dacombe, John 65, 66, 101
Dacombe, Mary 101
Dacombe, Zilpah Gwendoline
  63
Danesbury 20
Dare, Sister 98
Dean, Austen 67
Dean, William 19
Deanery Estate 18, 53
Deans Grove 20, 44, *54*, 109
Digby, Edith 98
Digby family 116
Digby, Mabel 98
Dingwall, Louie 113
Dinneth, Joseph 23
Dobb, Rev. W.L. 96
Dogdean Common 54
Dorset County Council 71, 77
Dorset Regiment 15
Drinkwater family 101
Drovers Cottage *14*, 15
Dumpton House 55
Dumpton School *54*, 55

Durham Light Infantry 33
Eighteen Acres 19-20, 26
Elliott's Grave 2, 106
Ellis Brothers 53, 63
Ellis, Charles 53
Ellis, Monty *13*
Elphinstone, Rev. Hon. Andrew
  4, 40
Emergency Water Supply 15
Fairfax, Lord Thomas 63, 81
Fairfield House 10
Farrant, Henry 25, *34*, 36
Fell, Kathleen 98
Fiander, Ron 75-6
Fire Brigades 25
Fish, George 11
Fitzmaurice, Ronald 112
Fletcher, Ronald 98
Flight Refuelling 20
"Flying Jeeps" 18
Football Club 7, 88, 90-1, 95,
  97, *102*, 109
Forestry Commission 81
Frampton, Cecil *71*
Frampton, Henry 52
Frampton, Jim *75*
Frampton, Mary 52
Frampton, Vera *75*, *85*
Freeman, Bob 76
Freeman, Margaret *75*
Fry, Percy 11
Further House 95
Gallop, Johnny 66
Garrard, Rev. Robert 111
Gas Works House 20
Gaunts Estate 54
Gaunts House 55
Genge, PC 35
Gillett, Mildred 77, 111
Girl Guides *88*, 98
Glen House 48
Glyn Estate 55, *102*
Glyn family 54, 82, 95
Glyn, Miss Carr 33

Hay, Maud 110
Hayeswood School 80
Hayward, Bob 73
Hayward, Reuben 66
Heathcote, C. 53
Hebditch, Kathy 72
Hebditch, Stan 72
Hewett, "Jimmy" 98
Hickes, Roly 115
High Hanger 47
Hillier, Dollie 72
Hillier, Winnie 71
Hillyer, Kathy 75
Hinton, Richard 76
H.M.S. Barham 29
Hoare, Ernie 79
Holder, Albert 85
Holder, Joyce 85
Holder, Ray 85
Holmsley Cottages 67, 88
Homer, Bob 13
Hope Cottage 24
Hopkins, Reubin 63
Horns Inn 7, 31, 44, 52-3, 55, 56, 62, 85
Horse and Jockey 22, 23
Horse racing 82
Howell-Evans, "Taffy" 78
Hunt, Percy 13
Hurd, Roy 106
Hyde, Frank 24
Iron Church 7, 92, 99, 109
Ivamy, George 63
Ivamy, Jane 63
Ives, F. I 108
Ives, F. II 108
James, Arthur 75
James, Jimmy 13
James, Mac 11, 13
Jeffrey, Rev. Michael 97
Jenkins, Harry 11
Jenkins, Maurice 11
Jenkins, Walter 73
Jenny Down 81, 91

Jockey Cottages 24
Jockey House 16, 21-2, 24-5, 27
Jockey Pond 22, 24
Jones, Alan 75
Jones, Andrew 98, 99
Jones, Janet 25
Jones, Ron 101
Joy, Reg 40
Joyce, Violet 13
Jupe, Audrey 68
Keable, Rupert 98
Keeping, Ken 13
Kemble, E.D. 32
Kerr, Lindsey 14
Kindersley, Mrs. 96-7
Kindersley, Rev. Cyril 55, 91, 95-6, 109
King, Jessie 71-2
King's Own Dragoon Guards 16, 121
King's, Richard, Close 19
Kingston Lacy Estate 16, 23, 56-7, 61, 68
Kingston, William 109
Lake, PC 35
Langer, George 31
Langer, Harry 30-1
Lawes, Winnie 11, 13
Lawrence, Barry 25
Lee, George 12
Lees, Bernarda 15, 29, 32-3, 42, 95, 97, 118, 119, 120
Lees family 118, 119
Lees, Thomas 118
Le Fleming, Sir Kaye 119
Legg, Donald 18
Legg, Doug 106
Legg, Violet 13
Leigh Arch 24
Leigh Common 16-9, 22, 23-7, 34, 36, 123
Leigh Farm 19-20, 22, 58
Leigh Manor House 21

Thorne, George II *73*, *95*
Thorne, Mabel *75*, *95*
Thorne, Nelly *74*, *95*
Tilley, Nell 101, 110
Top o' Cross 68
Tracy family 81
Trenaman, Florence 77
Trinity Chapel 77
Truell family 36, 47, 95, 121
Truell, Robert 47, 49, 92
Tucker, J. and Son 26
Uddens Estate 6, 16, 49, 67, 71, 79-82
Uddens Farm 69
Uddens House 63, 69, 71
United States "P.X." 41
Upper Leigh Farm 19-20
Vincecombe 19
Vine, Kitty 121
Vineries Football Club 11, *13*
Vincent, Sister 80
Walford Bridge 44
Walford Farm 44, 49
Walker, Margaret 28
Walker, Stanley 28
War Memorial 15, 28, 92, 99, 121
Wardle, Ray 77
Wareham, Edie *85*
Wareham, Ernie *73*
Wareham, Frank 88
Water Tower *43*, 44, 46-7
Watson, Garth 55
Watson, June 80
Way, Ernest 47, 121
Webb, Charles 28
Webb, Minnie 28
Webber, PC 106
Weedon, Stanley 98
Welch, Frederick 23
Welch, Jim 47

Welch, John 47
Welch, Reg 47, 65-6, *108*
Wentworth, Ken's, workshop 21
West, Reg *40*
West, Thomas 63
Weston, Jack 106
White, Albert 53
White, Dolly 72
White, Edith 68
Whitmarsh, Bert *13*
Wierzbicki, Alexander 114
Willcox, Reginald 33
Williams, Derek 19, 25
Williams, Garney *87*, *98*
Willis, B. 24
Willis, "Granny" 18
Willis, Marjorie *75*
Willow Cottage *113*
Wills, A.R. 9
Wimborne Drama Club 112
1st Wimborne Minster Boy Scouts 27
Wimborne Minster Girls' School 77
Wimborne Minster Water Works Company 44
Wingreen 47
Winton, Harris *42*, *43*
Women's Institute 7, 98
Women's Institute Choir 75
Woodman, Henry 20
Woodman, James 20
Woodman, John 20
Woodman, William 20
Woodward Survey 19, 48, 53, 56
Worley, F.A. 53
Wrigley, Bob 53
Wyatt, Ruth *13*